JAGUAR

·THE COMPLETE WORKS ·

JAGUAR
· THE COMPLETE WORKS ·

NIGEL THORLEY

For a man who appreciates the best — a book about the best.

Keith & Sylvia
October 1997

Published 1996 by Bay View Books Ltd
The Red House, 25-26 Bridgeland Street
Bideford, Devon EX39 2PZ, UK

© Copyright 1996 Bay View Books Ltd
Type and design by Chris Fayers & Sarah Ward
Design consultancy by Peter Laws
Edited by Chris Rees

ISBN 1 870979 69 9
Printed in China
by Leefung-Asco Printers Ltd

CONTENTS

INTRODUCTION

Grace... Space... and Pace are perhaps the three words that best epitomise a Jaguar. The phrase was coined in the postwar period to idealise the cars produced by Jaguar: vehicles created for a car-hungry society that wanted something more than the run-of-the-mill but at a more realistic price than the established quality marques.

Jaguar itself only became established as a marque in its own right after the Second World War. Previously known as SS Cars Limited, its existence stemmed from 1931, and earlier still it had its humble beginnings in the 1920s in Blackpool, Lancashire.

The real story of Jaguar Cars therefore starts back in 1921 with the meeting of a couple of like-minded motorcycle enthusiasts, William Walmsley, an emigrant to Blackpool from Stockport in Cheshire who was already manufacturing sidecars in his parents' garage at this time, and William Lyons, the son of an established Blackpool family.

At the age of only twenty 'Bill' Lyons was much younger than Walmsley, and it was his enthusiasm that soon warmed Walmsley to the idea of putting his motorcycle sidecar manufacturing on a proper businesslike footing. With financial assistance from both fathers, the two Williams started business in 1922 under the name The Swallow Sidecar Company, initially operating from very small premises in Bloomfield Road, Blackpool.

With Lyons' flair as an entrepreneur the sale of side-cars thrived, the best known being the Bullet, built around an ash frame with aluminium panels and echoing the Zeppelin style. A modest £28 would purchase such a quality sidecar back in the early 1920s. With sales booming the need for larger premises became acute, so extra space was taken in Back Woodfield Road and John Street, followed by a complete relocation to Cocker Street in 1926 which gave Swallow the capability to expand operations into specialist body building and repairs. Encouraged by the success of the Austin Seven, Swallow paid out £112 for a rolling chassis from a Bolton dealer. A stylish new body was designed and built, and duly launched in 1927, with the name Austin Swallow, as a drophead coupé at £175 and a fixed-head coupé at £185.

The new Swallow-bodied Austin was an instant success and was followed one year later by the even more stylish saloon version. Expansion of the body building side of the business was underwritten by a formal weekly order for the vehicles from the Henlys Group.

How it all started from Lyons, Walmsley and the Swallow Sidecar and Coachbuilding Company: a late-model Bullet aluminium sidecar attached to a Brough Superior motorcycle, a favourite of William Lyons.

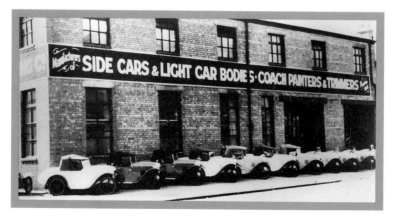

The first significant premises in Cocker Street, Blackpool, were owned by Swallow from 1926. Here sidecars were built alongside Swallow-bodied Austin Sevens.

The two partners realised the need to move premises yet again, this time into the heart of the motor industry in The Midlands in order to gain access to adequate materials and skilled labour, and so in 1928 the company moved lock, stock and barrel to Foleshill and a 40,000sq ft factory. Production increased from 12 to 50 cars per week, which included specialist Swallow bodies on other chassis including Morris, Swift and Standard.

The firm's connection with the Standard Motor Company commenced a relationship that would prosper until the late 1940s. William Lyons negotiated to purchase modified examples of the Standard Nine and Sixteen rolling chassis for the building of new cars designed by Swallow. These cars were to be the first SS models, and although there has never been any confirmation of what exactly these initials stood for, it is thought that, as far as William Lyons was concerned, they stood

THIS PLAQUE IS IN MEMORY OF
WILLIAM LYONS
WHOSE SWALLOW SIDE-CAR COMPANY,
LATER TO BECOME JAGUAR CARS
OCCUPIED THESE PREMISES 1926-1928
JUNE 1985

for Swallow Sports (and from Standard's point of view Standard Swallow!).

In the autumn of 1931 the new cars were released to the public, named SS 1 and SS 2. With rakish, low-slung styling, exceptionally long bonnets and a very high standard of equipment they certainly looked impressive, and were described in the press as The Dream Cars with the £1000 look, though selling for a very attractive £310 and £210 respectively.

With its profits approaching £38,000 in 1934, the business was reconstituted as a public company under the title of SS Cars Limited. William Walmsley, however, was not happy with the way the company was developing and, after losing interest, was bought out by Lyons, who effectively gained total control of the company's destiny.

The year 1934 also saw the company's first 'proper' Motor Show appearance with its own stand. Swal-

Present-day plaque at the Cocker Street works (top) commemmorates Lyons' early achievements. The first Swallow body on a contemporary Austin 7 chassis (above) launched the company on the path to Jaguar. The SS saloon (below) set Jaguar going while, behind it, the XJ12 Sovereign kept Lyons' design and engineering genius alive into the 1990s.

low-bodied cars were still being produced up to this time in relatively small numbers, as were sidecars, although by then both were taking a back seat to SS car production, which was growing apace. During the mid-1930s, derivatives of the original saloons were introduced and a combined total of nearly 5000 cars in the range was produced.

The 1930s also saw the introduction of a new saloon bearing for the first time the model name of Jaguar, selected from an exhaustive list of animal names to represent the type of car Lyons wanted to produce.

Introduced in 1935, the Jaguar took the motoring press by storm at its release at the Mayfair Hotel in London. It was based on modified Standard running gear, and was a sleek black four-door saloon with a 103bhp six-cylinder 2½-litre engine, twin carburettors, and an abundance of leather and woodwork. The assembled gathering was asked to price the new model but no one guessed as low as the £385 Lyons had set for the car. Although sceptics condemned Lyons and SS Cars

Sir William Lyons, for half a century the genius behind Jaguar, with his wife, Greta.

SS Cars Ltd launched the Jaguar name at the London Mayfair Hotel in September 1935 at a press lunch. This is the new SS Jaguar 2½-Litre saloon.

head coupé models were also introduced, boosting production further. A grand total of 14,000 of these cars were produced up to the beginning of the Second World War.

SS Cars Limited also launched a limited production range of sports cars in the late 1930s. First was the SS 90, built around a shortened SS 1 chassis and never widely publicised; only 23 were built prior to the introduction in 1935 of the SS 100 models in 2½- and 3½-litre form. Offering an improved performance over the saloons, the short-wheelbase two-door sports cars were designed in the contemporary sports car mould and offered exceptional value for money for their performance and specification.

At only £465 the SS 100's 125bhp engine gave a 0-60mph time of only 10.4 seconds, but only just over 300 SS 100s of all types were produced up to the outbreak of war, and the cars were not made post-war, making them today highly collectable and valuable.

Up to the outbreak of war SS Cars Limited pro-

saying that he could never produce it at such a low price – he did, and offered a 1½-litre version at only £295 as well!

With a full order book, Lyons could not hope to produce enough cars in the traditional coachbuilt manner, with ash framing, so with the aid of various companies he introduced the manufacture of all-steel bodywork from 1938. Production levels increased to over 200 cars a week after serious early problems in assembly. During this time the 1½-litre engine was increased in capacity to improve performance and a new additional 3½-litre version became available, offering a genuine 90mph performance from its 125bhp Standard engine. Handbuilt two-door drop-

duced a grand total of 20,000 cars in eight years, no mean feat for any automobile manufacturer let alone one that did not exist until the late 1920s. The profits yielded put the company in a good position for the postwar period.

During the war the factory was turned over to military work, which included repairs to Whitley bombers and the manufacture of parts for Stirlings, Mosquitos, Spitfires and Lancasters. Sidecars were also produced, around 10,000 being specially made for military use.

In 1944 the sidecar side of the business, by then known as Swallow (1935) Limited (after the resignation of William Walmsley), was sold off to the Helliwell Group (later Tube Investments) which continued to produce sidecars and eventually turned out the Swallow Doretti sports car based on the Triumph TR2 chassis.

In February 1945 the company wisely changed its name to Jaguar Cars Limited and Jaguar became a marque in its own right. (The initials SS at that time had unfortunate connotations.)

On September 21st 1945 car production got under way again, and Jaguar, like other car manufacturers of the time, began by resurrecting prewar designs. Lyons was able to purchase from Standard the tooling to produce the 2½- and 3½-litre pushrod ohv engines in-house; Standard retained the tooling for the 1½-litre engine as this was to be used to power new models in the Standard-Triumph range.

A factory fire in 1947 set back production momentarily but in the same year the company made its first exports to the United States, vital

Inside the legendary Browns Lane works in the late 1950s (top). Then it was one of the longest assembly lines in Europe and, even today, it is still used to produce X-300 saloons and XJS models. The disastrous fire of 1957 (above) destroyed hundreds of cars, including Mark 1s, Mark VIIIs, XKs and – most tragically – D-types. It was a major setback for Jaguar.

postwar era. After the war development continued, along with the designing of a brand new chassis and front independent suspension, also for the new luxury saloon.

By 1948 the chassis was complete and ready for production, as was the front suspension; but the engine still required further testing, while the new bodywork for the saloon was so complex that further work by Pressed Steel Fisher was needed before production of it could begin.

Lyons accordingly decided to launch the new chassis and suspension in an interim saloon model known as the Mark V (the designation reflected the fact that this was the fifth prototype). Although reminiscent of the pre-war designs, every panel was different, as was the interior trim. However, the pushrod engines were carried over and, at £1263 for the larger engined model, the Mark V was very well received.

during this period to ensure supplies of steel from the Government.

Prices of the Jaguar saloons had changed dramatically since the war, the 3½-Litre saloon now retailing for a massive £991. Yet sales went well and around 12,000 cars of the pre-war designs were to be produced up to 1948, when Jaguar introduced new models.

During the war the now celebrated engineering team from SS Cars Limited – Heynes, Baily and Hassan, plus William Lyons – spent many hours on fire-watching duties discussing and designing a new engine of advanced design to power a new saloon for the

As for the new advanced engine, this had been developed in both four-cylinder and six-cylinder form, the former making its debut in September 1948 powering the Goldie Gardner special to a record 176mph in Belgium.

Later that year, at the Motor Show in London, Jaguar launched a limited production run sports car featuring the new engine (now designated XK) as the XK100 (four-cylinder) and XK120 (six-cylinder). The smaller-engined car never in fact entered production, but the XK120 took the world by storm. The clamour of its reception turned into an embarrassment for

William Lyons as he had not planned to produce what was essentially a concept car in great numbers.

After only 200 had been produced with hand-built aluminium bodies, the factory had to tool up for full-scale all-steel production to cope with the outstanding orders and, by the end of 1953, a total of over 12,000 XK120s had been produced.

The success of the XK120 encouraged the company to enter competition with the car. This came to fruition in 1951 with the introduction of the XK120 C-type with specially designed bodywork by Malcolm Sayer. The success of the C-type – particularly in the Le Mans 24 hour race during the early 1950s – helped to establish Jaguar worldwide as a reputed manufacturer of fast quality cars. Lyons made every effort to capitalise on this success.

The competition side of the business was taken over by a young man who joined Jaguar Cars in 1946 as Service Manager. F.R.W. (Lofty) England was not only to play a major part in Jaguar's competition successes in the 1950s but would also eventually become Jaguar's Chief Executive following William Lyons' retirement.

In 1950 Jaguar launched the new top-of-the-range saloon for which the new engine and chassis were originally destined. The Mark VII saloon, as it was known, was a major force in the advancement of the company and remains to this day a vastly underrated model.

The fully enveloping bodywork incorporated elements of the XK120 wing line and was of mammoth proportions. With all the luxury equipment expected of such a saloon, the Mark VII offered the discerning buyer everything he could wish for at the exceptionally low price of £988. With the superb 160bhp XK engine, lavish wood veneering and Vaumol leather upholstery, the Mark VII was a match for anything else in the market place at the time, including the standard steel Bentleys and Rolls of the day.

The Mark VII was ideally suited to the North American market, still very important to any British manufacturer, and a large proportion were exported. With later modifications including the availability of auto-

Strike: difficult times for Jaguar at the launch of the XJ12 in 1972 as the factory closes down through industrial dispute.

matic transmission, sales totalled over 30,000 in less than six years.

By 1950 the Jaguar Foleshill factory was bursting at the seams, despite an expansion of the floor space to over 600,000sq ft. Lyons was able to purchase the ex-Daimler shadow factory near Allesley in Coventry to provide Jaguar with a total of 1 million sq ft of space, on the promise that it would continue with military contracts. By this time the company was exporting 84% of all its production, making it the country's largest dollar-earner in the USA.

Jaguar's racing success continued with the development of a new sports-racing model, the D-type, lifting the company's profile even higher. By the mid-1950s Jaguar Cars employed over 4000 people.

1956 was a highly significant year for Jaguar. Firstly William Lyons was knighted for his work in the motor industry and secondly the company introduced a brand new model to the range – the 2.4-Litre saloon. This crucial new model employed monocoque construction and was a less expensive (£1298) and smaller alternative to the gargantuan Mark VII. The model prospered with the introduction of a 3.4-Litre version in 1957, the addition of disc brakes on all four wheels and by successful appearances in saloon car racing and rallying. This was Jaguar's most prolific model to date, a total of over 37,000 2.4s and 3.4s being produced by 1959.

Perhaps the most momentous event of the period was the unfortunate major fire at Browns Lane on February 12th 1957, when several hundred cars were destroyed and production temporarily suspended. Due to the good offices of the workforce, the suppliers, competitors and to the single-mindedness of Sir William Lyons, the factory was back in production within a few days.

By the end of the 1950s Jaguar had produced over 138,000 vehicles, putting it in an enviably stable financial position; but if the 1950s had been a successful decade, the 1960s would turn out to be a true boom period.

The company was again in urgent need of more space

and in 1960 put in a successful bid to purchase the Daimler Car Company Limited, also based in Coventry. Part of Daimler's assets was a large factory at Radford, only a couple of miles away from Browns Lane. Daimler, although a well-respected manufacturer of cars, limousines, commercial and military vehicles, had suffered badly through a lack of sufficient capital to develop new models and did not enjoy the economies of large scale production which Jaguar did.

Purchased at a price of £3.4 million, the acquisition provided Sir William Lyons with expanded production facilities and an increase in the total workforce to over 8000, not to mention the stature of the Daimler name in his portfolio. Further acquisitions were soon to take place – the commercial vehicle manufacturer Guy Motors Ltd of Wolverhampton in 1961, and in 1963 Coventry-Climax, manufacturers of fork trucks and race engines, as well as the Henry Meadows organisation, all extending the Lyons empire.

The 1960s were to witness the introduction of many new models and in particular two of the most significant cars in the history of the company. At the end of 1959 came a revised version of the compact saloon, designated the Mark 2. This was offered in no less than three engine configurations, with prices starting from £1530. The version with the largest – 3.8 – engine was to earn the accolade of being the fastest production saloon of its day and would fare well in competition. It would also prove popular with local police forces around the country. Over 92,500 Mark 2s would be produced during the 1960s, making it the most successful Jaguar saloon ever until the XJ Series.

The other major new model arrived in March 1961 at Geneva with the unveiling of Jaguar's new sports car, the E-type. With style to better anything in its day the E-type at just over £2000 offered 150mph performance with sophisticated mechanicals and would prove to be the most widely appreciated Jaguar ever.

Nearly 93,000 E-types would be made in various forms from 1962 to 1975, and arguably it has since been the most coveted Jaguar, with a following span-

The research and development facility at Whitley, near Coventry, where Jaguar's products have been designed since the mid-1980s.

ning four generations. It is doubtful whether any mass-produced sports car since that time has had the same mystique as the Jaguar E-type.

The model range developed dramatically through the 1960s, with three versions of the Mark 2 (and later a further two), three Series of E-types in closed and open forms, a brand new flagship saloon from the end of 1961, the Mark X (later 420G), the mid-range S-type and 420 saloons and of course the Daimlers.

Although initially retaining the existing Daimler models – SP250 sports and Majestic Major saloon (plus the limited production limousine) – Jaguar saw the benefit of using the famous Daimler name to develop a range of models to compliment the Jaguars. In 1962 came the Daimler 2.5-litre V8 (based on the Mark 2 bodyshell but with subtle styling changes and the renowned Turner-designed Daimler V8 engine), the badge-engineered Daimler Sovereign based on the 420 saloon and then in 1968 the all-new DS 420 limousine, finished initially at Vanden Plas coachworks in London and employing many components of the Mark X/420G Jaguar.

Between 1960 and 1968, Jaguar managed to turn out over 230,000 cars until the introduction of the one-model policy with the XJ6 saloon. During the early 1960s Jaguar Cars Limited was still very much a William Lyons company: he owned 260,000 of the total 480,000 shares, with a Board of Directors totalling 25. Significant changes, however, were afoot when on 11th July 1966 Lyons engineered what he considered to be an important development to secure the future of the British motor industry with the merger of Jaguar Cars Limited (and its subsidiaries) with the British Motor Corporation to form a new conglomerate called British Motor Holdings Limited (BMH).

In 1968 Lyons relinquished his position as Managing Director of the Group (although he retained his title as Chief Executive) and F.R.W. 'Lofty' England became Joint Managing Director along with Robert Grice. In May of that year a further merger of BMH with the Leyland Group formed the British Leyland

Motor Corporation (BLMC).

Within four months of this merger Jaguar was ready to release the brand new XJ6, which quickly replaced all other Jaguar and Daimler saloons except for the DS420 limousine. Voted Car of the Year for 1969, the model went from strength to strength and proliferated into a wide range of models wearing both Jaguar and Daimler badges.

1972 was Jaguar's Jubilee Year and was marked by several major events. That year saw the launch of the high performance V12 engined version of the XJ saloon (which also became Car of the Year and was undoubtedly the fastest production saloon in the world at the time). The same year Sir William Lyons retired, leaving 'Lofty' England to take over as sole M.D.

In October of that same year Jaguar ceased to be a separate company within British Leyland and in 1973 Geoffrey Robinson became Managing Director by agreement with Lord Stokes. 'Lofty' England himself retired in the following year.

At this time Jaguar's annual output amounted to some 30,000 cars and its image was suffering under the creaking regime of British Leyland. In particular, Jaguars of the period were of very poor build quality. And, as part of the Leyland corporate body, Jaguar even lost its independent sales force, leading to the formation, in the late 1970s, of the 'luxury' car division Jaguar-Rover-Triumph Limited, an entity which lasted only a couple of years.

During Jaguar's 'grey' period, the XJ continued to develop despite the difficulties and in 1975 a brand new two-door grand touring coupé based on the saloon arrived, the XJS. Significantly different in style from anything that had gone before, the XJS was met with mixed reactions but over the years gained a strong reputation.

The renaissance of Jaguar Cars Limited came at the beginning of the 1980s through the vision of a new head, John Egan (later knighted for his work). Substantial effort was put into both quality of assembly and the quality of parts sourced from outside suppliers, while the V12 engine was redesigned to improve economy. The company's new image was promoted under the banner 'The Legend Grows'.

Two classic Jaguars beside the overhauled multi-million pound Browns Lane assembly line in 1993. These cars are now in the Jaguar-Daimler Heritage Trust's hands.

Sir John Egan negotiated the purchase of the Castle Bromwich body plant to make Jaguar completely independent. Millions of pounds were invested in computerised body assembly and new methods of painting, and in revitalising the network of dealerships.

Both the XJS and the Series 3 XJ saloons received a new lease of life with hundreds of improvements and the addition of new models. During this time Jaguar was not sitting on its laurels, for the development of the next generation of saloons was well under way.

Sir John Egan announced the privatisation of the company in 1984. This proved to be a great success as the shares were vastly over-subscribed. Jaguar Cars Limited regained its independence and, with guaranteed protection against takeover, the company prospered. Reflecting its new-found confidence, the board of directors redeveloped the Browns Lane assembly site and built a brand new research, development and engineering centre at Whitley.

1986 saw the launch of the all-new XJ6 (code named XJ40) which put Jaguar back in the forefront of luxury car production. Voted Car of the Year, the XJ and its derivatives improved Jaguar's sales dramatically whilst the XJS continued with minor modifications and two new variants, the Cabriolet and Convertible.

The takeover protection afforded by the Government's 'Golden Share' in Jaguar ran out in 1990, by which time rumours were rife about takeovers from BMW as well as General Motors, but eventually it was Ford which took overall control of Jaguar in 1991.

Despite many reservations at the time about the takeover, Jaguar prospered under Ford control. During the recessionary years of the early 1990s the company regained its market share with extra models based on the XJ40 saloon and a major investment in a new assembly line at Browns Lane to increase production capacity in the future. More recently the brand new XJ Series (code-named X-300) has put Jaguar firmly back in the luxury car race with increased levels of refinement, build quality and dynamic ability.

The continuing development of completely new models for the rest of the 1990s and into the 21st century looks set to guarantee the future of the Jaguar marque.

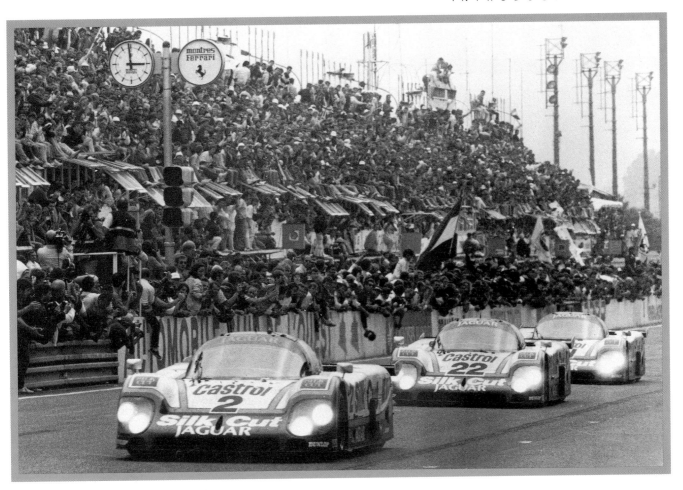

A Jaguar enthusiast's dream: a three-car finish at Le Mans with the XJR-9 in 1988.

Jaguar extremes: Swallow sidecar beside XJ220 supercar.

CHAPTER ONE

SS 1 & SS 2

1931-36

SS1

Following his successful launch into the world of four-wheel motoring via the Swallow-bodied cars, William Lyons negotiated a deal with John Black of The Standard Motor Company to purchase a suitably modified version of the then current Standard Sixteen chassis. Standard's own running gear and the 16hp 2054cc and 20hp 2552cc straight-six sidevalve units were chosen for the new Lyons-designed cars.

Although Lyons and his then partner William Walmsley disagreed over the final design of the cars, they turned out to be rakish, sporty and with an up-market air which belied their price. At 14ft 6in long the low slung two-door coupé looked bigger and much more powerful than it really was, an impression enhanced by the elongated bonnet, which accounted for over half the total length of the car. Period helmet wings covered wire wheels, while an imposing frontal aspect was created by a plated grille and bumper and substantial headlights with a plated tie-bar. The roof and boot area was covered in fabric to add that further touch of luxury.

Inside, the SS 1 was particularly well equipped, with leather upholstery, wood trim, sculptured seating and

Original concept drawing of the SS 1 (above) exaggerates the low-slung bodywork and long bonnet of the first SS sports car. Compare the concept drawing with the real thing (below), the 1931 SS 1 2-Litre. Dumb irons, fabric-covered boot, cycle wings, wire wheels and long bonnet helped the SS 1 look like twice its actual price of £310.

such touches as a rear window blind and companion set for the lady.

The SS 1 was not a fast motor car by any stretch of the imagination. In fact it took a 16hp version over 20 seconds to achieve 50mph from standstill and its maximum speed was only just above 70mph, providing you could stand the vibration and the very restricted vision from the small windscreen over that enormous bonnet. Yet the car looked right and certainly appeared to the uninitiated as if it would out-perform other much sportier machinery of the day.

On its launch for the 1932 model year, the SS 1 Coupé was heralded as a car which looked like £1000 but cost only £310. This price represented exceptional value for money when compared to anything else on the market at the time. The SS 1 could stand alongside the likes of the contemporary Alvis and Lea-Francis on the golf club car park without looking out of place, even if its performance left a little to be desired.

In 1933 the Fixed Head Coupé was joined by a second variant, the Tourer, which provided four-seat accommodation but with the added advantage of a fold down hood and windscreen and sporty cutaway doors. In reality the Tourer was merely a cut-down version of the Coupé.

Fabulous art-deco styling for the 1935 SS 1 Airline was surely the prettiest of any SS model. Twin side-mounted spares, swept rear-end treatment and virtually pillarless side glass were excellent features.

Magnificent interior of this SS 1 Airline had unpleated leather trim, much use of wood and dials from the SS 90 sports car.

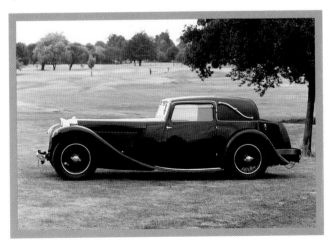

Engines for the SS range derived from Standard. This is the 2-litre six-cylinder engine used in the SS 1.

A very elegant two-light saloon on the SS 1 chassis, with handsome chrome-rimmed Rudge-Whitworth wheels.

The much more evenly proportioned lines of the restyled SS 1 of 1934 (above) with its swept-back wings, more extensive use of chrome, and greater space and airiness for rear seat passengers. Rarest of all the SS 1 types was the Drophead Coupé (below), of which only 94 were built. The hood folded away into a special compartment in the boot area.

By the end of 1933 William Lyons had totally redesigned the SS 1 so that it was more to his liking, a brand new chassis having an extra seven inches in the wheelbase. The Standard engines also came in for modification, with capacities increased to 2143cc and 2663cc and, as well as many other mechanical changes, the body style was totally updated.

Taking advantage of the extra wheelbase, the passenger compartment was also made larger and instrumentation revised. The exterior styling was substantially improved with a better proportioned roof area, swept back wing treatment and many other detailed refinements including a stylish metal cover for the spare wheel. The new SS 1 increased slightly in price to £335, for both the Coupé and the Tourer.

For 1934 another model joined the range: the Four Light Saloon. At £340 the Saloon was virtually identical in specification to the Coupé. The dummy hood irons were replaced by a further window on each side, making the car much more airy inside and improving visibility for the rear seat passengers. This substantially increased its attraction as a proper four-seater.

By 1935 the model range had expanded further with the addition of the Airline saloon and a Drophead Coupé, making a total of five styles of coachwork on the SS 1 chassis. The Airline remains to many the most stylish of all the SS 1 models with entirely new coachwork featuring a curved rear roof section, twin side-mounted covered spare wheels set into the front wings, horizontally louvered bonnet sides and a pillarless window treatment. The attractive Airline enhanced the rest of the SS 1 range although Airline sales were limited to a mere 624 overall.

At £360 the Airline was not, however, the most expensive SS 1 produced. This accolade went to the last and rarest of the SS 1s, the Drophead Coupé at £380, of which only 94 were ever produced. The Drophead Coupé offered saloon car comforts (including wind-up windows) but with the benefit of a fully retracting hood that could be stowed away out of sight inside the top-hinged trunk. The design concept of the Drophead Coupé was very much in the mould of the Rolls Royce Phantom 2 Continental and other up-

market drophead styles of the 1920s and 1930s.

The SS 1 continued into 1936, during which time prices of all models were reduced by up to £20 to help clear stocks which had built up due to the release of the brand new SS Jaguar saloons. A total of 4229 SS 1s were produced.

SS 2

A smaller version of the SS 1, the SS 2 was released at the same time in 1931 and featured virtually identical styling, albeit scaled down to an overall length of only 12ft.

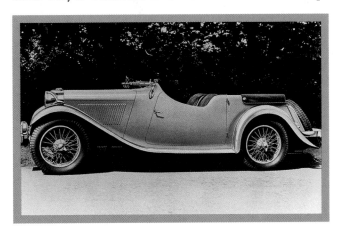

The four-seater Tourer version of the second generation SS 1 (above left) had cutaway doors, a collapsible hood and folding windscreen, but was otherwise identical to the saloon. Rather unbecoming treatment for the SS 2 dash (above right) with hexagonal instrument surrounds. SS 1 Tourer (below): an early example of William Lyons' work being pressed into police service. Jaguars would remain a favourite of constabularies across Britain right up to the present day.

Shorter and with two-light bodywork, the SS 2 of 1931 was not as pretty as the SS 1, and a lot slower.

S P E C I F I C A T I O N S

SS 1 (1931-33)

Engine: 2054cc/2552cc six-cylinder sidevalve, Solex carburettor
Bore & stroke: 65.5 × 101.6mm/73 × 101.6mm
Power output: 45bhp/55bhp at 3800rpm
Transmission: Four-speed manual
Wheelbase: 9ft 4in (284cm)
Length: 14ft 6in (442cm)
Width: 5ft (152cm)
Height: 4ft 7in (139cm)
Weight: 21cwt (1067kg)
Suspension: Front/Rear: beam axle, half elliptic leaf springs
Brakes: Bendix cable operated
Top speed: 70mph (112kmh)
0-50mph (80kmh): 20 secs (2054cc)
Price new: £310 (Fixed Head Coupé)

SS 1 (1933-36)

As SS 1 (1931-33) except:
Engine: 2143cc/2663cc six-cylinder sidevalve, RAG carburettor
Bore & stroke: 65.5 × 101.6mm/73 × 106mm
Power output: 53bhp/68bhp at 3800rpm
Wheelbase: 9ft 11in (302cm)
Length: 15ft 6in (472cm)
Width: 5ft 5½in (166cm)
Height: 4ft 7in (139cm)
Weight: 27cwt (1371kg)
Top speed: 77mph (123kmh)
0-50mph (80kmh): 19 secs (2143cc)
Price new: £325 (Fixed Head Coupé)
Total Production: Fixed Head Coupé 1810;
Four Light Saloon 1144; Tourer 551; Airline 624;
Drophead Coupé 100 **Grand Total** 4229

SS 2 (1931-33)

Engine: 1006cc four-cylinder sidevalve
Bore & stroke: 60.25 × 88mm
Power output: 28bhp at 4000rpm
Transmission: Three-speed manual
Wheelbase: 7ft 6in (228cm)
Length: 12ft (366cm)
Width: 4ft 6in (137cm)
Height: 4ft 6in (137cm)
Weight: 13cwt (662kg)
Suspension: Front: beam axle, half elliptic leaf springs.
Rear: live axle, half elliptic leaf springs
Brakes: Bendix cable operated
Top speed: 60mph (96kmh)
0-50mph (80kmh): 27 secs
Price new: £210

SS 2 (1933-36)

As SS 2 (1931-33) except:
Engine: 1343cc four-cylinder sidevalve
Bore & stroke: 63.5 × 106mm
Power output: 32bhp at 4000rpm
Transmission: Four-speed manual
Wheelbase: 8ft 8in (259cm)
Length: 13ft 8in (416cm)
Width: 4ft 8in (142cm)
Weight: 20cwt (1016kg)
Top speed: 62mph (100kmh)
0-50mph (80kmh): 26 secs
Price new: £260
Total Production: Fixed Head Coupé 703;
Four Light Saloon 905; Tourer 186; Van 2
Grand Total 1796

The post-1933 version of the SS 2 shared the flowing wing treatment of its larger brother. These examples are a four-light saloon with sunroof (above) and a four-seat tourer (below).

Based around the Standard Nine chassis complete with its 1006cc four-cylinder engine married to a three-speed gearbox, the little SS 2 developed a very modest 28bhp so it could only manage a top speed of around 60mph with a 0-50mph time of a little under 30 seconds.

Priced at £210 and initially available only in Coupé form, the SS 2 offered reasonable value for money in a quality package for the motorist who didn't need the extra bulk or speed of the SS 1 but who still required a distinctive style of car to set him apart from the rest. The SS styling, however, did not look as convincing on this shorter wheelbase model.

After only a few months the SS 2 gained a four-speed gearbox and, by the end of 1933 (after the introduction of the revised SS 1), the smaller car was also substantially modified. Abandoning the Standard Nine chassis in favour of SS's own adaptation, the wheelbase was extended by a massive 13in, increasing the overall length of the car by 20in. The engine was replaced by a new 1343cc version of the Standard unit which boosted power to 32bhp, and there was the option of an even larger 1608cc engine for only £5 extra!

Thus the SS 2 became a full four-seater with styling changes similar to the SS 1. The price was increased to £260 while a new saloon (four light) version was offered at £265. A limited production Tourer also came on the scene at the same price as the Coupé and in 1935 SS even produced two vans! It is believed, however, that these commercial vehicles were only ever used by the factory and were later destroyed.

Despite the many changes to the SS 2, the model was never as successful as the larger SS 1 and a total of only 1,796 SS 2s were produced up to the demise of the model in 1936.

S S   9 0   &   S S   1 0 0

1 9 3 5 - 3 9

1935 prototype (above left) for the SS 90 shows established lines of thought, although the rear end would be substantially reshaped. The production SS 90 (above right) with its squarer tail section. The stubby rear wings distinguished it from the later SS 100. SS 90s are extremely rare today, only 23 ever having been made.

SS 90

The first true sports car to be produced by SS Cars Limited was the SS 90, launched to the public in March 1935, very much as a competition model for those who saw the SS's potential in racing and rallying. The model attracted a great deal of attention as it was a total departure from anything Swallow or SS had previously produced and the '90' designation indicated the car's top speed of 90mph, a very attractive feature at the time and one offered by few other road cars.

Of course the SS 90 was based on the SS 1 models but on a shortened version of the chassis with a wheelbase of only 8ft 8in (1ft 3in shorter than the SS 1) whilst retaining the same track. The mechanicals followed the SS 1 exactly although the SS 90 was only ever available with the 2663cc (70bhp) engine equipped with twin RAG carburettors (which had also been adopted for the SS 1 by this

time). The principal advantages of the shorter wheelbase were lightness, manoeuvrability and a reduced turning circle of 35ft 6in.

Bodily the SS 90 echoed the classic sports car lines of the 1930s with swept back wings, large headlights, prominent grille and strictly two-seater accommodation. A shortened version of the SS 1 radiator grille surround was used, with a honeycomb fret effect instead of slats; in front of this was a full size stone guard, also chromed. A lowered, louvred bonnet was fitted which provided improved vision for the driver and better cooling for the engine.

At the rear end the hood folded away behind the front seats, giving a clear view behind. The rear end treatment on the original prototype featured in contemporary magazine articles showed a sloping tail with a flush fitting spare wheel. However, on production models an exposed slab fuel tank accommodated a bolt-on protruding spare wheel.

SS 90 interior showing the curved dash top, folding windscreen and attractive gauges. The speedo doubled up as a rev counter.

From the front, larger headlamps, recessed grille and different badging were all that told an SS 100 apart from its short-lived predecessor. It was more powerful, however, and could reach a genuine 100mph. This car has optional aeroscreens to supplement the standard fold-flat windscreen.

The launch price of the SS 90 was only £395, making the car very competitive as a sports car. Because the model had a very short life span (1935 only) a total of only 23 were built before the introduction of the much improved SS 100.

SS 100

In September 1935, coinciding with the introduction of the new Jaguar saloons, SS also announced a revised version of the SS 90 sports car, the SS 100, although sales did not actually begin until 1936.

Revisions to the saloon chassis, including new Burman worm steering and Girling rod brakes in enlarged drums, were carried over for the SS 100. With the advantage of a Weslake designed cylinder head and

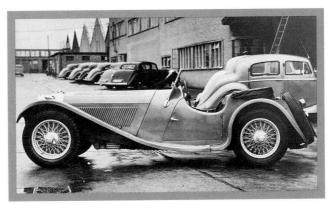

There is something about the shape of the SS 100 which encapsulates 1930s sports car themes. This is an original example pictured at the SS works.

twin SU carburettors, the output of the SS 90's 2½-litre engine was significantly increased to around 104bhp. This, along with the improved steering and brakes, made the SS 100 far more of a sports car and justified the new designation '100', indicating that the car could very nearly reach the magic ton.

In the styling department the SS 100 retained the basic appearance of the '90' but differed at the front with new headlights, a revised recessed grille, '100' badging and a winged motif bearing the inscription 'SS Jaguar' on the radiator grille top. At the rear the difference was more apparent with a Le Mans style fuel tank and spare wheel inclined at an angle.

At 23cwt (slightly heavier than the '90'), the SS 100 delivered a fair turn of speed, with a 0-50mph time of

Simplicity, elegance and purposefulness combined to make the SS 100 one of the best-looking sports cars ever.

Hood-up (above left), the SS 100's profile suffered. Note the Le Mans style fuel tank and angled twin spare wheels. At speed in the SS 100 (above right), the enthusiast owner was virtually assured that there would be nothing else on the road to approach his pace.

8.8 seconds and a genuine maximum of between 95 and 100mph. At the same price as the '90' (£395), the SS 100 was a bargain!

By September 1937 major revisions were taking place at SS brought about by the change-over to all-steel bodywork. With these changes came a stiffer chassis for all models including the SS 100, whose price remained unchanged.

The big news for the '100' was the introduction of a larger engined version of 3½ litres capacity (3485cc) to be sold concurrently with the 2½-litre car. Still based around Standard's own unit, the 3½-litre engine was redesigned by Heynes of SS with a bore and stroke of 82 and 110mm respectively and a cylinder head based on the head designed for the 2½-litre engine by Harry Weslake. Twin SU carburettors, a multi-branch exhaust manifold and a seven-bearing crankshaft with steel connecting rods guaranteed much better performance and running capabilities.

An output of 125bhp was boasted for the new SS 100 engine and, in road test conditions, the car achieved a 0-60mph time of 10.4 seconds and a genuine 100mph maximum speed. A higher rear axle ratio of 3.8:1 was fitted for 3½-litre engined cars.

The 3½-litre SS 100 cost £445 and, like the 2½-litre version, remained in production only until the outbreak of the Second World War, by which time only just over 300 examples of all engine sizes had been delivered.

Today the SS 100 is highly regarded and much sought after by Jaguar enthusiasts, since the car represents the first of a long line of great Jaguar sports cars.

This SS 100's dials (above) had black-on-white faces. Note the separate rev counter and the speedo calibrated to precisely 100mph. The twin-carburettor 3½-litre engine is pictured below.

S P E C I F I C A T I O N S

SS 90 (1935)

Engine: 2663cc six-cylinder sidevalve
Bore & stroke: 73 × 106mm
Power output: 70bhp at 4500rpm
Transmission: Four-speed manual
Wheelbase: 8ft 8in (259cm)
Length: 12ft 6in (381cm)
Width: 5ft 3in (160cm)
Height: 4ft 6in (137cm)
Weight: 22½cwt (1143kg)
Suspension: Front: beam axle, half elliptic leaf springs.
Rear: live axle, half elliptic leaf springs
Brakes: Bendix cable operated drums
Top speed: 89mph (142kmh)
0-50mph (80kmh): 12 secs

Price New: £395
Total Production: 23

SS 100 (1935-39)

As SS 90 except:
Engine: 2663cc/3485cc
Bore & Stroke: 73 × 106mm/82 × 110mm
Power Output: 104bhp at 4600rpm/125bhp at 4250rpm
Length: 12ft 9in (388cm)
Weight: 23/23¼cwt (1168/1181kg)
Brakes: Girling rod operated drums
Top speed: 95/101mph (150/162kmh)
0-50mph (80kmh): 8.8/7.1 secs
Price new: £395/£445
Total Production: 2½-litre 191; 3½-litre 118 **Grand Total** 309

CHAPTER THREE

SS & JAGUAR SALOONS
1935-48

September of 1935 saw the launch of 'Jaguar' as a model name for the very latest SS saloon models. Of the new saloons, *The Motor* magazine said in 1935: 'With distinguished appearance, outstanding performance and attractive price as the main characteristics, the new SS Jaguar range represents an achievement of which Mr. Lyons and his technical staff may well feel proud.'

When first shown to the press at an extravagant dinner at the Mayfair Hotel, no-one could believe the prices of the saloons: £295 for the 1½-litre version and £385 for the 2½-litre car. The saloons used a modified SS 1 chassis, widened and stiffened by virtue of boxing in the perimeter members and incorporating repositioned rear springs. The braking system was also of the new Girling drum 'transverse wedge' type.

As for the larger engined car, the biggest advance was a new version of the well-tried Standard 2½-litre engine specially adapted by Weslake with an overhead valve arrangement, new manifolding and twin SU carburettors which increased output to a maximum of 104bhp at 4600rpm.

The smaller engined car used the Standard Twelve sidevalve engine of 1608cc as adapted for the SS2. Offering a maximum power output of around 52bhp with the aid of a single Solex carburettor, the little SS was still good for more than 70mph. Other aspects of the mechanicals were the same as the larger engined car save for the smaller diameter drum brakes and a chassis cut down to 11ft.

Perhaps the single greatest attribute of the new SS Jaguars, however, was the styling. The four-door four light coachwork broke new ground for SS: of distinguished appearance and well proportioned, it could easily have been mistaken for a coachbuilt Bentley or Alvis of the period. These SS Jaguars had an air of majesty about them, with well proportioned dimensions, a brand new dominant radiator grille style, Lucas P100 headlights, a 'built in' curved boot area and even a spare wheel

The large saloons offered by SS during the 1930s were sporting yet traditional. This 1935 1½-Litre (top) had a shorter bonnet than its 2½ and 3½-Litre sisters, otherwise there was nothing to distinguish them externally. On the 1937 SS 2½-Litre (middle), the longer bonnet is self-evident. From 1936, all SS saloons had quarterlights in the front windows and the door handles were sited in the chrome waistline strip. Compare this 1938 model SS (above). It had a thinner chromium waistline, which indicates that it is one of the cars built with 8in longer all-steel bodywork.

side mount for the nearside front wing. At 14ft 10in in length (13ft 11in for the 1½-litre – the reduction all taken from bonnet length) and 5ft 7in wide (5ft 11½in for the 1½-litre), the SS Jaguar looked significantly bigger.

Internally the SS Jaguar was also a match for other more established and well respected contemporary saloons. The door panels carried the distinctive 'sunrise' pleating of previous SS models, there was plenty of leather and walnut veneer and enough space to accommodate four to five people in comfort. Standard equipment included a metal sliding sunroof, opening windscreen, well equipped dashboard, an adjustable steering column and even an extensive tool kit fitted in the boot lid.

By 1937 the SS Jaguars were selling exceedingly well and modifications started to appear. Firstly, the chassis was modified to allow extra width in the rear compartment and the fitment of a larger rear seat and side mounted arm rests. Front door opening quarterlights improved ventilation and a separate wiper motor permitted the fitment of more modern windscreen wiper mechanisms. Other improvements included the fitment of larger brake drums, better carburation and air cleaning, and an automatic choke system.

The traditionally built body of steel and alloy panels on an ash frame limited the factory's production

A high degree of comfort awaited the passengers in an SS saloon. Leather and walnut veneer abounded.

Just as well proportioned from the rear as from any other angle. This is an all-steel 3½-Litre saloon, as made from 1938.

Impressive toolkit was a standard fitment in a compartment in the boot lid.

capacity and, after intensive development, an all-steel body of slightly changed proportions was adopted for production from the 1938 model year.

The switch over to all-steel construction affected most other aspects of the car, including a more rigid chassis which was spot welded to form box sections with 6in deep side rails and revised spring mountings. However, the new design retained the existing Burman steering and Girling brake systems virtually unchanged.

The adoption of all-steel construction and the new chassis brought with it certain changes to the body style. Firstly the cars looked sleeker because they were longer – 8in on the larger engined cars and 6in on the 1½-litre version. Aesthetically, the line of the bonnet louvres and front doors were angled to match the slope of the windscreen, and gone was the side mounted spare wheel, initially to a hidden position in the boot lid and later to a special compartment below the boot accessed via a separate cover.

The increased length was incorporated entirely within the wheelbase, allowing extra room in the interior, wider seating, a flat floor, more space for rear seat passengers and better access for the driver and front seat passenger thanks to redesigned doors.

The ex-Lady Lyons SS Jaguar 1937 2½-Litre saloon (above), still in original condition and owned by Jaguar to this day. Note the delightful covered side-mounted spare wheel. The 2½-litre engine (below) was the mid-range power unit in the SS Jaguar saloons. It developed 104bhp and could power the car up to a top speed approaching 90mph.

Simple yet effective styling for the 1937 SS saloon interior.
The 'sun ray' pattern on the door trim was an SS trademark.

The SS radiator badge design effectively conveyed the
marque's sporting character.

Drophead coupés joined the revised saloon range in 1938.

The 2½-litre engine remained substantially unaltered for the new model which was priced at £395. The 1½-litre model, however, received a brand new engine of 1776cc taken from the Standard Fourteen, modified by SS with an overhead-valve head (replacing the side-valve unit), which increased its output to 65bhp at 4600rpm. The new head – again designed by Weslake – also featured a four branch exhaust manifold and single SU carburettor. The 1½-litre SS Jaguar was still the 'loss leader' for the company, retailing at the very attractive price of under £300.

Another new engine was also to feature in the SS Jaguar saloon models. The 3½-litre (3485cc) engine,

still manufactured by Standard, used the bottom end from the 2½-litre block with steel connecting rods plus a cast iron deep-section cylinder head with overhead valves and a separate alloy water rail running the whole length of the head, and finally special manifolding and twin 1½in SU carburettors.

The 3½-litre engine developed no less than 125bhp in the saloon on a 7.2:1 compression ratio. Thus it achieved excellent performance figures: a 0-50mph time of only 9 seconds and a claimed top speed in excess of 90mph. And the price of all this luxury and performance was a mere £445.

Not content with the three SS Jaguar saloons (plus

Styling drawing for the SS 2½-Litre Drophead Coupé, taken from contemporary company literature, emphasises its elegance.

the SS 100 sports car), William Lyons went one step further by offering hand-built two-door drophead coupés based around the saloon shell. Although of the same overall design as the saloon cars, the dropheads featured the traditional construction technique on an ash frame to provide stiffness to the body without the need for a steel roof section. The two front opening doors were wider than on the saloon to allow easier access to the rear seating area.

A complex hood arrangement made from mohair and horsehair mirrored the contours of the saloon roof and featured substantial hood irons; the two-position hood allowed a sedanca style arrangement as well as the more normal fully-folded position, when the hood could be covered with a tonneau. Only a small degree of head room was lost, while the seat back was moved more upright to accommodate the furled hood. The increased cost of specifying a drophead coupé was not outrageous at £20 for the 1½ and 2½-litre versions and £50 for the 3½-litre model.

The SS Jaguars continued virtually unchanged until the outbreak of the Second World War except that, for the last few months of production in 1939, the horns were re-sited to a position hidden beneath the front valance, the spare wheel carrier at the rear was enlarged and all models featured as standard what SS called 'air conditioning' which was in reality nothing more than a fresh air heating system with a demister. Other interior changes included simplified door trims, non-pleated seating and the provision of veneered picnic tables in the backs of the front seats.

The SS Jaguar saloons had proved to be the most successful vehicles yet produced by Swallow and SS, a grand total of over 14,000 being made up to the outbreak of war.

POSTWAR DEVELOPMENTS

In 1945 production of the pre-war saloons recommenced but, since the company name had changed to Jaguar Cars Limited, the cars now featured the name Jaguar (not SS) on badging, manuals and brochures.

Despite restrictions on raw materials, Jaguar was able to recommence production of exactly the same range of cars as pre-war except for minor alterations to some inner steel panels, thinner chrome waist strips, slightly altered radiators (including new insignia) and new 'Jaguar' spinners for the wire wheel hubs.

Mechanically very little changed: the four-cylinder engine benefited from improved breathing while the manufacture of the 2½- and 3½-litre six-cylinder engines came completely under the control of Jaguar, as William Lyons had successfully negotiated the purchase of the required tooling from Standard. The braking system was also modified and, for the first time, left-hand drive became available on all saloons.

Perhaps the most significant change, however, was the pricing of the postwar models. The 1½-litre saloon increased to £386, the 2½-litre saloon to £494 and the 3½-litre to a massive £546.

The drophead coupés – still relatively hand built – did not re-enter production until 1947 and only continued until the end of 1948, whereas the saloons soldiered on into the beginning of 1949, despite the introduction of a brand new saloon a few months earlier.

Over and above the 14,000 pre-war SS Jaguar saloons and dropheads, nearly 12,000 more were made during the postwar period. The pre- and postwar SS Jaguar saloons made a substantial contribution to the company's profitability and established Jaguar as a manufacturer of high quality luxury saloons.

Drophead coupé coachwork by Maltby has shallower windows and longer tail.

SPECIFICATIONS

SS 1½-LITRE SALOON (1935-37)
Engine: 1608cc four-cylinder sidevalve
Bore & stroke: 69.5 × 106mm
Power output: 52bhp at 4300rpm
Transmission: Four-speed manual
Wheelbase: 9ft (274cm)
Length: 13ft 11in (424cm)
Width: 5ft 1½in (156cm)
Height: 5ft (152cm)
Weight: 21cwt (1067kg)
Suspension: Front: beam axle, half elliptic leaf springs. Rear: live axle, half elliptic leaf springs
Brakes: Girling rod operated drums
Top speed: 70mph (112kmh)
0-50mph (80kmh): 19.6 secs
Price new: £295

SS 1½-LITRE SALOON (1938-48)
Engine: 1776cc four-cylinder overhead valve
Bore & stroke: 73 × 106mm
Power output: 65bhp at 4600rpm
Transmission: Four-speed manual
Wheelbase: 9ft 4½in (286cm)
Length: 14ft 5in (439cm)
Width: 5ft 5½in (166cm)
Height: 5ft (152cm)
Weight: 26½cwt (1346kg)
Suspension: Front: beam axle, half elliptic leaf springs. Rear: live axle, half elliptic leaf springs
Brakes: Girling rod operated drums
Top speed: 72mph (115kmh)
0-50mph (80kmh): 17 secs
Price new: £298
Total Production: 1½-litre saloon 12,452; 1½-litre dhc 677
Grand Total 13,129

SS 2½-LITRE SALOON (1935-48)
Engine: 2663cc six-cylinder overhead valve
Bore & stroke: 73 × 106mm
Power output: 104bhp at 4600rpm
Transmission: Four-speed manual
Wheelbase: 9ft 11in (302cm) early/10ft (305cm) late
Length: 14ft 10in (452cm) early/15ft 6in (472cm) late
Width: 5ft 7in (170cm)
Height: 5ft 1in (155cm)
Weight: 31cwt (1575kg) early/32cwt (1626kg) late
Suspension: Front: beam axle, half elliptic leaf springs. Rear: live axle, half elliptic leaf springs
Brakes: Girling rod operated drums
Top speed: 87mph (139kmh)
0-50mph (80kmh): 10.6 secs
Price new: £385
Total Production: 2½-Litre saloon 6778; 2½-Litre dhc 383
Grand Total 7161

SS 3½-LITRE SALOON (1937-48)
Engine: 3485cc six-cylinder overhead valve
Bore & stroke: 82 × 110mm
Power output: 125bhp at 4500rpm
Transmission: Four-speed manual
Wheelbase: 10ft (305cm)
Length: 15ft 6in (472cm)
Width: 5ft 6in (168cm)
Height: 5ft 1in (155cm)
Weight: 32cwt (1626kg)
Suspension: Front: beam axle, half elliptic leaf springs. Rear: live axle, half elliptic leaf springs
Brakes: Girling rod operated drums
Top speed: 92mph (147kmh)
0-50mph (80kmh): 9 secs
Price new: £445
Total Production: 3½-litre saloon 4925; 3½-litre dhc 801
Grand Total 5726

CHAPTER FOUR

MARK V

1948-51

Although it looked rather like the SS Jaguar saloons, the Mark V body was entirely new. Wire wheels were never offered.

The automobile industry after the Second World War was at first totally dependent on prewar designs, but soon every manufacturer was clamouring to produce new models and Jaguar was certainly no exception.

Jaguar's technicians had already been working on a brand new engine to power the flagship saloon of the 1950s along with a fresh chassis which featured new independent front suspension and all-new bodywork. But development of the new bodyshell and engine in the postwar austerity years took longer than Jaguar would have wished, preventing an early launch of the new saloon; yet Jaguar needed something new to sustain sales and keep customers interested. So an interim model was announced towards the end of 1948, dubbed the Mark V, the designation

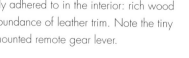

Tradition was strictly adhered to in the interior: rich wood veneers and an abundance of leather trim. Note the tiny floor-mounted remote gear lever.

merely signifying the fifth prototype of the model.

At first glance the uninitiated might confuse the Mark V with any of the previous SS and Jaguar saloons from 1935, and indeed it was directly derived from them, inheriting the 2½- and 3½-litre straight six overhead-valve engines. (The Mark V was never offered with the smaller 1½-litre engine as the tooling for this unit had been retained by Standard for use in its own cars.)

The Mark V also carried the same transmission as the older cars except for a divided propshaft. However, underneath that traditional styling lay something entirely new. The 'old' drive train had been installed in a brand new prototype chassis (which would become the basis for the all-new Mark VII). Developments on this new chassis allowed Jaguar to accommodate into the Mark V a

Perhaps the Mark V's best angle was the rear three-quarter view, showing off the harmony of its proportions and the flow of its lines.

The Mark V confirmed the Jaguar qualities of 'Grace, Space and Pace'. New features under the skin were independent front suspension and hydraulic brakes.

new independent front suspension system conceived for the Mark VII.

The new chassis was formed of massive box section side members of 6½in depth and 3½in width, straight in both planes to eliminate torsional deflection. These side members rose sharply at the rear over the rear axle, allowing increased axle movement and more flexible suspension. At the front a heavy box section cross-member ensured rigidity and a solid base for the independent front suspension. Extra stiffness to the chassis was provided by cruciform central cross-members through which the divided propshaft passed, allowing a flat floor for rear seat passengers.

The lower wishbone of the independent suspension comprised an I-section beam into which the silico-manganese torsion bar was splined, reinforced by a tubular strut running from the outer end diagonally and attached on the front cross-member to take braking loads. The stub axle assembly swivelled in special self-adjusting ball joints at the outer ends of the wishbones, the joints also forming the outer articulation of the suspension. Girling telescopic shock absorbers ran directly upwards from the lower wishbone to a bracket above the chassis.

To accompany the new package Jaguar fitted smaller all-steel 16in rim wheels of 5in width shod with specially manufactured Dunlop Super Comfort tyres and finished with attractive chrome hub caps and rimbellishers. Along with the stiffness of the new chassis and the independent front suspension, this gave the Mark V significantly improved handling capabilities over the previous model and a smoother ride. Rear springing was also softened for the Mark V.

Steering remained virtually unchanged from the old

An imposing grille the equal of any pre-war SS graced the Jaguar Mark V, seen here in a placement with the police, who found its combination of performance, keen handling and spaciousness ideal for their purposes.

The chassis first used on the Mark V would form the basis for a whole generation of separate-chassis Jaguars lasting until 1961.

models although amendments were made to ensure the Mark V could cope with the up-and-down motion of the new independent front suspension, although the new car suffered an increase in lock-to-lock turns from 2.5 to 3.25. Hydraulic brakes by Girling featured for the first time on any SS or Jaguar via a single master cylinder and 12in drums all round.

Aesthetically, Jaguar hedged its bets with very conservative styling, belying the fact that it was actually all-new. No panel was interchangeable with the old model. Unmistakably a Jaguar from the rear and from the front (particularly the even more imposing radiator grille), the Mark V played to the export markets with an abundance of brightwork, substantial bumpers, faired-in headlights and push-button door handles.

At only 1in longer and 3in wider than the old model, the Mark V did look more imposing, especially with its increased glass area and the narrow chrome-on-brass window frames which improved vision for the driver and passengers.

Internally it was a case of 'all change' with a new dashboard and instruments and the now-famous 'black violet' reflective lighting. There was new seating without pleats but still in quality Vaumol leather, and increased rear passenger room, helped in no small measure by the flat floor.

The same power units were used but overall weight rose by 1cwt, so the Mark V was slightly slower than the model it replaced. The 3½-litre was nearly one second slower to 50mph but there were big improvements in driveability.

Launched at a price of £1247 for the 2½-litre and £1263 for the 3½-litre model, the Mark V represented excellent value for money being very fully equipped, even including standard fog lamps and a sunroof.

Lowering the hood of the Drophead Coupé involved unfurling the front section to a sedanca de ville position, then folding the hood irons. The result was an unparalleled luxury touring car.

To compliment the saloons Jaguar also introduced two-door drophead coupé versions as before, although these reached the market place a few months after the introduction of the four-door saloons. Relying heavily on the old design, the bodies were still virtually hand built utilising a lot of ash framing and wood strengthening, and the dropheads were by far the most attractive of the Mark V designs. These were available with the same engine options as the saloons and, despite the extra work involved, prices were exactly the same as the saloons.

Mark Vs also found favour in competition circles. They came home 3rd and 9th in the 1951 Monte Carlo Rally and 3rd in class in the 1952 RAC Rally.

In many ways the Mark V was a testbed for the Mark VII chassis and suspension. Despite the fact that many knew the Mark V was a stop-gap model, it sold well both in the UK and overseas with a total production run of just under 10,500, the 3½-litre versions actually running alongside the Mark VII production line until June 1951.

SPECIFICATIONS

MARK V (1948-51)

Engine: 2663cc/3485cc six-cylinder overhead valve
Bore & stroke: 73 × 106mm/82 × 110mm
Power output: 104bhp at 4600rpm/125bhp at 4250rpm
Transmission: Four-speed manual
Wheelbase: 10ft (305cm)
Length: 15ft 7in (475cm)
Width: 5ft 9in (175cm)
Height: 5ft 2½in (159cm)
Weight: 33cwt (1676kg)
Suspension: Front: independent, wishbone, torsion bar, anti-roll bar. Rear: live axle, half elliptic leaf springs
Brakes: Girling hydraulic drums
Top speed: 87/97mph (139/155kmh)
0-50mph (80kmh): 11 secs/10 secs
Price new: £1247/£1263
Total Production: 2½-litre saloon 1661; 2½-litre dhc 29; 3½-litre saloon 7831; 3½-litre dhc 972
Grand Total 10,493

CHAPTER FIVE

XK120

1948-54

Unmistakably a Jaguar, the XK120 Roadster was the original and purest of the XK series. Its shape was both aerodynamic and exquisitely unadorned.

I f ever a Jaguar could be classed as revolutionary it was the XK120 sports car of 1948: it broke entirely the mould of the typical British sports car. Achieving significant moves forward in comfort, ride, style and mechanics, the XK120 offered the sports car driver probably the best combination of performance, handling and style of any car in the world but at the unbelievably low price of £998 plus purchase tax.

The XK120 was a development of the work carried out for the new 'flagship' saloon of the 1950s, the Mark VII, and to some

The heart of the XK120 was its brand new XK engine, an absolute benchmark in the history of engines. Powerful, smooth and flexible, the six-cylinder unit would power many successive generations of Jaguars.

extent could be considered the equivalent of a 'concept' car. Never intended for mass production, the new sports car utilised a shortened version of the Mark VII chassis (used in the Mark V interim saloon discussed in the last chapter) with the same independent front suspension, braking system and other mechanical components, except that is for one very big difference.

Development during and after the war had concentrated on a brand new engine to power the Mark VII, under the designation 'XK'. Of bold design more reminiscent of contempo-

The dramatic lines of the XK120 Roadster look like they have been hewn from a single piece of metal. The Roadster is easily identified by its cutaway doors without handles.

Although starker than other XK models, the Roadster's interior (right) was still luxurious by the standards of the day, with leather seats and dash, carpets and a full complement of instruments.

An XK120 Roadster is not often seen with its hood and sidescreens in place (below): after all, they were mere items of convenience. Body-coloured wire wheels were an option.

The Drophead Coupe offered all the comfort and convenience of the Fixed Head but with a fully convertible roof. Unlike the Roadster's hood, it was designed to be left permanently on the car.

rary high performance, ultra expensive, Italian machinery, the XK engine took the motoring world by storm.

Twin chain driven overhead camshafts in an all aluminium head, hemispherical combustion chambers with inclined valves and central sparking plugs, lightweight webbed cast iron block, massive seven bearing counterbalanced crankshaft, twin branch exhaust manifolds and twin 1¾in SU carburettors all added up to an impressive package. And it looked the part, too, with vitreous enamelled exhaust manifolds and polished alloy cam covers.

The engine was rated at 160bhp at 5000rpm from its capacity of 3442cc which meant that, in the 25½cwt bodyshell, the XK120 could easily better the 120mph to which the model number alluded, while there was acceleration to match – 0 to 50mph in under 7½ seconds.

The bodyshell was hand formed in aluminium with simple yet effective rakish lines. Little adornment was necessary and even the thin chromium-plated bumper bars looked like an after-thought. A non-traditional plain oval radiator grille without bonnet mascot emphasised the XK120's priorities: simplicity and speed. Unusually, the grille formed part of the bonnet and lifted alligator fashion for unrivalled access to the engine bay.

The body styling took many of its cues from the SS 100 and SS Jaguar saloons and included full spats over the rear wheels reminiscent of the newly introduced

Mark V model. Initially only a roadster version was available with a removable hood and, in the time-honoured sports car tradition, the two cutaway doors sported separate side screens.

Inside the cabin the simplicity continued with a relatively plain fabric covered dashboard featuring all the usual instrumentation and, although the seats were trimmed in Vaumol leather (sometimes in two-tone colour schemes), none of the traditional Jaguar woodwork veneer was to be found anywhere.

Strictly a two-seater, the XK120 was not the most comfortable of cars with its near-vertical and somewhat over-powering Bluemels steering wheel and a dearth of interior space. Yet it drove in a refined manner more akin to that of a saloon car – and all this from a sports car with excellent road manners and a fine turn of speed. Despite its sportiness and compactness there was also a reasonable boot, making the XK120 a true grand touring car.

At launch time the XK120 was one of two XK sports cars announced by Jaguar, the other being a four-cylinder version known as the XK100. Effectively using a cut-down version of the XK six-cylinder engine (still retaining twin overhead camshafts), the smaller engine had a capacity of 1995cc and developed 95bhp. The XK100 might have proved a successful model had it not been for the XK120 which completely over-shadowed it in performance terms. On price the XK100 would have sold at almost exactly the same figure as

With its hood raised, the Drophead Coupé looked elegant and was completely waterproof, at least in theory. It also had proper winding windows, saloon-type quarter lights and exterior door handles.

the XK120, so it never in fact entered production.

There was overwhelming demand for the XK120, which proved to be an embarrassment to William Lyons as the car was never intended for series production. It was presented as a handbuilt car for production in limited numbers, at the same time serving as a platform for Jaguar's new engine. Jaguar soon realised that the number of orders being received from day one far outstripped the manufacturing capability of a car built in aluminium, so Pressed Steel set about tooling up for an all-steel body. Only 200 alloy-bodied XK120s had been produced when, in mid-1950, the steel-bodied versions came on stream. Only slight alterations to the curvature of the panels differentiated the alloy and steel-bodied cars although the latter weighed in at around 1cwt heavier.

By March 1951 Jaguar had released an alternative to the XK120 roadster in the form of a proper Fixed Head Coupé. Cleverly designed so that the fixed head roof matched the profile of the Mark V/VII saloons, the fixed head offered full saloon car comfort. Wind-up glass windows in chrome-on-brass frames, opening front quarter lights, exterior door handles and locks, veneered dashboard and luxury headlining were only some of the refinements of the new model. Priced at just £1088, the Fixed Head proved a worthwhile and popular addition to the XK range, boosting sales still further.

Initially all XK120s were available only with steel

wheels but by the autumn of 1951 wire wheels, either in body colour or in silver, became a popular option. With wire wheels fitted the full spats at the rear were removed. At the same time an improved cylinder head boosting power to 180bhp also became available to special order.

In April 1953 a further XK120 derivative was offered in the form of a Drophead Coupé with a new hood beautifully executed in mohair. The advantage over the roadster was the one-man operation to raise and lower the hood in situ and the provision of fixed head comforts like wind up windows and wood veneer. At only £1160 the Drophead Coupés maintained the value-for-money theme of Jaguar's range of sports models. In production for the shortest period of all the XK120s, the Drophead Coupé was easily the rarest variant.

Also in 1953 a close ratio gearbox became available and, to very special order, you could have an engine fitted with the new C-type cylinder head, which boosted power up to over 200bhp.

All three XK120 models remained in production until September 1954 when they were superseded by the next generation, namely the XK140. In the six years of the model's life over 12,000 XK120s were produced, confirming Jaguar as one of the major players in the sports car manufacturers club. On another level, the XK120 was to spur Jaguar into action on the competition front, described in the next chapter.

A Jaguar advert (right) celebrating the debut of the XK120 in 1948 at Earls Court. The public was staggered by the car's appearance and specification. For its part, Jaguar was taken aback by the level of orders for what was intended to be a limited production model.

The Fixed Head Coupé (below) is inevitably regarded as the poor man of the XK family but it was unusually handsome, practical and comfortable. The shape of the rear pillars echoed the strong contours of the Mark V saloon.

All XK120s were strict two-seaters. The Drophead Coupé offered more luxury and comfort than the Roadster, but it weighed more.

The Drophead and Fixed Head had a more opulent feel about their interiors, with walnut veneer on the facia and door cappings, and a standard glove box.

S P E C I F I C A T I O N S

XK120 (1948-54)

Engine: 3442cc six-cylinder twin overhead camshaft
Bore & stroke: 83 × 106mm
Power output: 160bhp at 5000rpm/180bhp at 5300rpm (Special Equipment)
Transmission: Four-speed manual
Wheelbase: 8ft 6in (259cm)
Length: 14ft 5in (439cm)
Width: 5ft 2in (157cm)
Height: 4ft 5½in (136cm)/4ft 4½in (133cm) Roadster windscreen

Weight: 25½cwt (1295kg)/27 cwt (1372kg) Fixed Head
Suspension: Front: independent, wishbone, torsion bar, anti-roll bar. Rear: live axle, half elliptic leaf springs
Brakes: Lockheed hydraulic drums
Top speed: 120mph (192kmh)
0-50mph (80kmh): 7.5 secs
Price new: £1263
Total Production:
XK120 Fixed Head Coupé 2678; XK120 Roadster 7612; XK120 Drophead Coupé 1765
Grand Total: 12,055

CHAPTER SIX

C-TYPE, D-TYPE & XKSS

1951-57

The C-type's finest hour: Rolt and Hamilton on their way to victory in the 1953 Le Mans 24 Hours.

C-TYPE

The C-type sports/racing car was specifically conceived by Jaguar's technicians to win one race, the Le Mans 24 Hours held each year in France. Le Mans carried great prestige and Jaguar saw the opportunity to capitalise on this. With the successful launch and sales record of the XK120 sports car, completely standard models were entered for the 1950 event and they very nearly won! Lapping consistently well, the XK120s proved both their ability and their reliability.

William Lyons himself sanctioned the development and preparation of a revised XK120 for the 1951 Le Mans race as late as June 1950, and the fact that cars were ready for the following year's race was a tribute to the hard work and enthusiasm of the Jaguar team; work did not actually start on the car until October 1950 due to development pressures in other areas such as the Mark VII and steel bodied XK120s. Production

cars obviously took priority in a time of scarce resources.

Due to the dynamic prowess and known reliability of the XK120, Jaguar made few mechanical changes, instead concentrating on a new wind-cheating body and lowering the weight of the car to improve overall speed. However, some mechanical modifications were necessary. An improved cylinder head with larger 1⅝in exhaust valves and 1⅜in porting was fitted along with increased length valve springs and a new camshaft. Indium coated lead bronze bearings, high speed crankshaft damper, solid skirt pistons and a 9:1 compression ratio also ensured enhanced performance. Carburation was the same as on the standard XK120 (although for 1952 onwards 2in SUs were used), while there was an amended branched exhaust manifold. The net effect of all this was to increase the power output to 204bhp at 5500rpm.

For the transmission Jaguar stayed with the XK120

four-speed gearbox but with a one-piece input shaft to assist quick changes between ratios. A lighter flywheel and 10in Borg and Beck solid centre section clutch passed the power back through the gearbox to a Salisbury rear axle.

To keep weight to a minimum, Jaguar technicians abandoned the conventional XK120 chassis and instead used a new tubular steel framework stiffened in certain specific areas; the centre sections provided immense strength, being 10inches deep in section.

The Burman steering system of the XK120 was replaced with a more positive rack-and-pinion system which also gave a better feel. The front suspension included wider based wishbones, long torsion bars anchored by the scuttle, and Newton telescopic shock absorbers. For the rear suspension there were no leaf springs; instead there was a single torsion bar mounted transversely. All these revisions combined to produce a car that handled well and was liked by its drivers, particularly when driven on the limit.

The XK120 drum brakes had been the single biggest problem in the 1950 Le Mans race and so these came in for improvement in the C-type. The front Lockheed drums were adjusted automatically during driving to eliminate long pedal travel after hard use. To improve brake cooling, wire wheels were fitted. These had quick action knock-off splined hubs to speed up wheel changing. Dunlop racing tyres were fitted to improve grip.

Bodily the XK120 C-type took an entirely fresh approach. Of all-aluminium construction, the body was aerodynamically designed to cheat the wind and built with light weight as its top priority.

The front end of the new body was built up as a complete single section forming the bonnet, wings, radiator grille and lights. Hinged at the front, the whole front section swung forwards from the scuttle to allow unimpeded access to the mechanicals. The

The C-type's prototype engine bay. The XK engine was given a new head and camshafts, higher compression, higher lift valve springs and many other changes to yield over 200bhp.

same applied to the rear bodywork: a single piece was detachable via the minimum number of bolts to gain access to the rear suspension and axle. Even the supporting chassis framework was detachable by undoing a few bolts. A 40-gallon alloy fuel tank was sited over the rear axle and the spare wheel (a regulation fitment for Le Mans) was fitted in a special compartment within the rear bodywork.

Three C-types were entered for the 1951 Le Mans 24 Hour race, and the car driven by Whitehead and Walker took first place at an overall average speed of 93.49mph. The new model had proved its superiority on its very first outing. Continued success came with Stirling Moss in the TT Race at Dundrod when he broke the lap record, while other C-types came in 2nd and 4th.

Further development continued on the C-type for 1952, spurred on by the re-entry into racing of the famed Mercedes-Benz team. Experimental disc brakes were introduced into the C-type and, to achieve a higher maximum speed, all-new front and rear bodywork offered less resistance to the wind. At the front there was a new, steeply sloping nose section incorporating the headlights. For the rear, a similar treatment created a wedge shape necessitating the use of recessed lighting.

Along with slight mechanical changes, the cars were entered for the 1952 Le Mans 24 Hour race. But there had been insufficient testing and they had to retire early on with overheating problems, probably created by the new bodywork design, which had forced changes in the cooling system. By 1952 C-types were being made available to the newly formed Ecurie Ecosse racing team from Scotland.

The works Jaguar team started 1953 with revised cars. The SU carburettors were replaced by twin choke Webers, crankshaft damping was modified and stronger top piston rings fitted, while there was a new Borg and Beck triple plate clutch of 7¼in.

On the suspension side, the 1953 cars benefited

The C-type's all-aluminium body was both wind-cheating and elegant. Its exceptional speed and handling made it a natural choice for serious privateer racers in the early 1950s.

The XK engine looks familiar under the C-type's removable bonnet, but it has a special branched manifold. Note the tubular chassis frame.

Racing trademarks: bare aluminium inside the cockpit, the absolute minimum of instruments needed for competition work and a tiny wind deflector and aero screen.

from the fitment of a single cast torque arm and Panhard rod. Dunlop disc brakes on all four wheels became the norm for C-types along with hydraulic servo assistance.

In an effort to reduce weight further, many aspects of the cars were modified: the tubular frame was of a thinner gauge metal, the metal fuel tank was replaced by a flexible bag tank and a lighter battery was used in a new location. Lastly, the aerodynamic slopes of the bodywork were replaced by styling similar to that of the 1951 car.

The 'new' cars entered the Le Mans race yet again, up against arguably the strongest competition to date. Despite the stiff opposition and the haste in which the C-types were prepared, Jaguar won again.

After 1953 Jaguar no longer ran an 'official' team although it continued to assist the many privateers who raced C-types. Indeed the car had virtually achieved production model status, having its own brochure and a price tag of just over £2300.

Competition success fell like rain in spring for the C-type, which was *the* sports racing car to own and drive in the early 1950s. In total only 54 C-types were built and the vast majority survive to this day.

D-TYPE

Like the C-type, the 'D' was built specifically with Le Mans in mind and was born out of an experimental car prepared around a C-type which had achieved over 178mph in October 1953 at Jabbeke in Belgium.

Construction of the first D-type proper started in March 1954 using a surprising number of standard production parts, which eventually enabled it to be built on the Browns Lane production line.

Fundamentally the mechanical side was very similar to the C-type, the D-type running with an improved ride height by virtue of a vernier adjuster, while it used rack-and-pinion steering and improved brakes adapted from the earlier car.

Dry sump lubrication allowed a lower engine height, improving the aerodynamic potential of the bodywork as well as bringing down the centre of gravity. A more efficient cooling system was also seen on D-types as well as an all-new four-speed all-synchromesh gearbox. Improved manifolding and other modifications increased the power output to 250bhp at 5750rpm. Dunlop peg drive light alloy wheels were employed for their strength.

Whilst the D-type was mechanically more or less a very direct development of the C-type, the bodywork for it was all-new and technically very advanced. Designed by Malcolm Sayer with much use of a wind tunnel for model testing, the wind-cheating and futuristic shape of the D-type have made it a classic.

It was built around a central monocoque in aluminium with full length front-to-rear sills for added structural rigidity. A transverse box-section member gave strength to the front bulkhead and a further double-skinned bulkhead was used at the rear, eliminating the tenets of conventional chassis design. Bodywork at the rear was merely bolted on to the bulkhead for ease of disassembly and, as on the C-type, the front bonnet and wings formed a one-piece hinged section to ease access and removal.

The D-type's first outing was at Le Mans in 1954. Driven by Rolt and Hamilton, this battered car dropped out of the race after it had recorded the fastest speed on the Mulsanne straight.

The aerodynamic shaping of the nose section incorporated faired-in headlights and a grilleless mouth to improve cooling to the engine. At the rear the last-minute addition of a tailfin behind

Business-like D-type interior, clearly showing the metal division between driver and passenger, wrap-around perspex screen and metal tonneau cover.

the driver's head was found to improve stability considerably. The whole redesign produced a body which was lighter than the C-type's.

The D-type's first outing was at the 1954 Le Mans where, due to reliability problems, the cars didn't win but at least managed to record the fastest time on the Mulsanne straight.

For 1955 various structural changes were made. The forward framework supporting the engine and suspension was made a separate bolt-on assembly and was built from lighter nickel steel rather than magnesium alloy. The rear end of the bodywork became a stressed skin for added strength and lightness; this also increased the ground clearance.

Five factory team cars also received attention to the frontal styling – lengthening the car by about 7½ inches to improve air penetration – and have since been referred to as the 'long nose' D-types. These cars were also given a full wrap-around windscreen and a new lengthened tailfin which extended to the extreme rear of the bodywork.

Mechanically, the 1955 cars featured re-worked cylinder heads and modified manifolds. Output was thereby increased to 270bhp at 5500rpm. D-types also went into production at this time and cars were offered for sale to private buyers at £3878, rather expensive perhaps but, considering how technically advanced the cars were and simply how fast they were (0-50mph was achieved in only 3.9 seconds), the price was of secondary importance.

For 1956 further modifications took place and the cars entered for Le Mans received lighter bodywork, front anti-roll bars and the benefit of Lucas electronic fuel injection. After that year Jaguar withdrew from racing due to pressure on manpower and manufacturing facilities for production cars. Private entries continued to flourish with the D-type, the main protagonists being the Scottish Ecurie Ecosse team.

Total production of the D-type amounted to a mere 68 cars, of which four were later dismantled for parts

In short-nose form (above), the D-type looked purposeful. Not all D-types had the long fin treatment: many were fitted with cut-down rounded fins. A short-nose D-type (below) in action at Goodwood in its heyday. The long tail fin was fitted because it helped directional stability

and five were destroyed in the 1957 fire. D-types won no less than nine major international events outright as well as a considerable number of placings. And they were instrumental in the development of Jaguar's most famed sports car of all, the E-type.

XKSS

The idea of a road-going D-type to be called the XKSS came about towards the end of 1956 in an effort to use up spare monocoques at the factory. Unfortunately production was to be cut very short due to a major fire at the factory in February 1957 and only 16 new cars plus two D-type conversions for private owners were ever made.

Modifications to the D-type included the removal of the rear fin and the metal division between driver and passenger, and generally improved accommodation, including leather trim and a nearside opening door for the passenger, who still had to step over a very hot side-mounted exhaust system!

To make the cabin more comfortable for road use, the XKSS was fitted with an adapted Ford Consul windscreen and surround and a folding hood with the luxury of fitted sidescreens. There was no facility for a proper luggage boot, merely a chromium-plated rack fitted atop the rear deck and, as a token gesture to protect the bodywork, neat chromed quarter bumpers were fitted, reminiscent of later E-types. All XKSSs were built with short-nose bodywork.

Mechanically the XKSS was identical to the D-type. It could accelerate from 0 to 60mph in a little over 5 seconds and do a standing quarter mile in 14.1 seconds, making it one of the very fastest sports cars in the world at that time.

This, the rarest of all production Jaguars, may not have been all that practical but who knows how successful the car could have been if the tragedy of the factory fire in 1957 had not brought to an abrupt end this exciting model's life. Fortunately most of the cars still exist and are among the most valuable of all classic Jaguars.

One of the first works D-types produced (above). This is a short-nose example. Snorting air intakes for the D-type's triple carb XK engine (right) boosted its power output as high as 270bhp. In long-nose form (below), the D-type had better cooling and wind-cheating qualities. However, wind-tunnel testing has subsequently revealed that the D-type is not especially aerodynamic.

A suburban setting for the XKSS (right) suited it better than the paddock. Makeshift hood, quarter bumpers, muffled exhaust, fixed side screens and an ungainly Ford Consul windscreen were the practical changes. The XKSS disguised its racing origins with a full dash (far right), cubby hole, no metal bar between driver and passenger and plenty of extra trim.

Extremely rare XKSS – only 16 were made – was the road-going version of the D, made from 'left-over' D-types.

SPECIFICATIONS

The following information refers to 'standard' production models – many cars were individually prepared to other specifications.

C-TYPE (1951-53)

Engine: 3442cc six-cylinder twin overhead camshaft
Bore & stroke: 83 × 106mm
Power output: 204bhp at 5500rpm
Transmission: Four-speed manual
Wheelbase: 8ft (244cm)
Length: 13ft 1in (399cm)
Width: 5ft 4½in (164cm)
Height: 3ft 6½in (108cm)
Weight: 20cwt (1016kg)
Suspension: Front: independent, wishbone, torsion bar, anti-roll bar. Rear: rigid axle, torsion bar
Brakes: Lockheed hydraulic drums
Top speed: 144mph (230kmh)
0-50mph (80kmh): 6.1 secs
Price new: £2327
Total Production: 54

D-TYPE/XKSS (1954-57)

Engine: 3442cc six-cylinder twin overhead camshaft
Bore & stroke: 83 × 106mm
Power output: 250bhp at 5750rpm to 270bhp at 5500rpm
Transmission: Four-speed manual
Wheelbase: 7ft 6½in (230cm)
Length: 12ft 10in (391cm)/13ft 10in (421cm) XKSS
Width: 5ft 5½in (166cm)
Height: 2ft 7½in (80cm)
Weight: 20cwt (1016kg)
Suspension: Front: independent wishbone, torsion bar. Rear: live axle, trailing links, transverse torsion bar
Brakes: Dunlop discs, triple pad front, double rear
Top speed: 162mph (259kmh)/149mph (238kmh) XKSS
0-50mph (80kmh): 3.9 secs/4.1 secs XKSS
Price new: £3878
Total Production: D Type 68; XKSS 16 **Grand Total** 84

CHAPTER SEVEN

MARK VII/VIII/IX

1950-61

Some regard the Jaguar Mark VII as one of the most important pieces of car design. Certainly its evolutionary styling was in perfect proportion and its lines fused purpose and dignity. From the front (below left), the Mark VII was simple to the point of severity. There was no heavily chromed grille surround, or any adornment to speak of. Room to move in the Mark VII (below right). Bench seat and two pedals identify this as an automatic model, a version which was not entirely successful, with only two speeds. Traditional veneered dashboard featured a full range of instruments.

Whilst Jaguar had found instant success with the XK120 sports cars there is no doubt that it was the saloons that sustained the company's profitability in the 1950s and 1960s and that one particular range of models, although consistently underrated, was highly significant in putting Jaguar on the map in the luxury car sector of the market – the Mark VII to IX saloons.

We have already mentioned the development of the new XK six-cylinder engine, the new chassis to accommodate it and the new independent front suspension, all of which found their way piece-meal into other models prior to the introduction of Jaguar's 'flagship' saloon for the 1950s.

The Mark VII (as the new saloon was to be known) acquired its model designation by default. The Mark V

On the move, the Mark VII was surprisingly fast and agile (above), while at the same time remaining composed and refined. It is perhaps the most underrated Jaguar of all. The simple beauty of the Mark VII's traditional British wood veneer dash (right).

With a significant boost in power, the Mark VIIM of 1954, below, was a better performer than its predecessor. Free-standing fog lamps, separate indicators, horn grilles and more wraparound for the rear bumper distinguished it.

should have given way to the Mark VI but Bentley got in there first! So, not wishing to cause confusion to luxury car buyers (and let's not mistake the fact that William Lyons dearly wanted to address Bentley owners), Jaguar opted to 'miss' a number and perhaps even contemplated getting one up on Bentley by selecting a higher number to indicate a superior model!

The styling of the Mark VII echoed the themes of the XK120, repeating the swept back front wings and full spats over the rear wheels. Even the radiator grille lost its prominence to some extent, making do without the usual heavy chromium surround. The styling of the roof line, with its chromium plated window frames, was carried over from the Mark V, leaving no doubt as to the parentage of the new Mark VII. Whilst the general style was more modern, with such features as forward-hinged front doors and an 'alligator' opening bonnet, the Mark VII still had a split windscreen.

The Mark VIII of 1956 was instantly recognisable by its heavier grille surround, chrome swage line and cutaway rear wheel spats. Two-tone paint schemes were common.

Built up from a complex set of panels produced for Jaguar by Pressed Steel, the Mark VII was a much bigger and more imposing car than the Mark V at over 9in longer, 4in wider and nearly an inch taller. Added to the fact that the engine was positioned 5in further forward in the chassis, the net result was extra legroom for rear seat passengers, wider seating, less intrusive wheel-arches and a much bigger boot area.

Interior appointments were totally revamped over the Mark V with a revised dashboard, new fully-pleated seating and the novel incorporation of tool kits in the front door trims.

Available only as a four-door saloon with manual transmission, the Mark VII was strategically priced at only £988 plus purchase tax, a staggering one-third of the cost of a standard steel-bodied Bentley saloon of the period! The Mark VII was also virtually unique in offering such a sophisticated engine in a saloon car package. A Drophead Coupé version was considered and Jaguar even built one example with an electric hood mechanism, but the concept never reached production.

Like the XK120, the Mark VII became an instant success, with record orders from North America. American motorists loved the combination of the traditional comfort and luxury of a quality British marque and sports car performance and handling.

If there was one major complaint from the Americans about the Mark VII it was the transmission: accustomed to their automatic 'slush boxes' they did not expect to have to change gear on a luxury car. Jaguar rectified this situation in 1953 with the launch of an automatic transmission option which employed the tried and tested Borg Warner gearbox, already well known in the USA.

Within the next few months, in January 1954, the manual transmission also became available with a Laycock de Normanville overdrive unit operating on top gear only. Along with a revised rear axle ratio, this permitted high speed cruising in a more relaxed manner, at the same time improving fuel economy.

The Mark VII not only found favour with private owners but turned out to be a force to be reckoned with on the competition scene, both in rallies and saloon car races. It acquired quite a reputation, even among the top drivers of the period.

Steady development improved the Mark VII throughout its life, perhaps the most significant change being the introduction of the Mark VIIM in September 1954. Although retaining the same basic mechanical specification and body style, a host of minor changes in nearly every department justified the change in model designation. Bodily the Mark VIIM received revised bumper bars and overriders which were simpler to manufacture and with better wrap-around at the rear. Gone were the flush-fitting fog lights in favour of pod-mounted Lucas types. Headlight units were also improved with the latest Lucas J700 units, the old fashioned trafficators were replaced by modern wing-mounted indicator lights and the lighting was also uprated at the rear. Additionally, rimbellishers became a standard fitment on Mark VIIM wheels.

Internally the Mark VIIM benefited from a revised flat horn push in the centre of the steering wheel. There was Dunlopillo cushioning for the seat interiors, slight amendments to the door trims and veneer cappings, while, on automatic transmission models, a full width bench front seat was fitted.

Mechanically the Mark VIIM featured standardised ⅜in lift camshafts which resulted in a power output of 190bhp (a significant increase of 30bhp), revised gearbox ratios and larger diameter torsion bars which reduced body roll.

By the time of the Mark VIIM's release, prices had inevitably increased, yet at just over £1600 the VIIM was still very competitive compared with other cars in this sector (£2100 for an Armstrong-Siddeley Sapphire, £2800 for a Daimler One-O-Four, £5000 for a Bentley).

This particularly startling all-white scheme is a rare example of a Mark VIII painted in a single colour. Only 6000 Mark VIIIs were produced before the Mark IX arrived.

MARK VIII

The Mark VIIM continued in production until July 1957 but, from October 1956, it was joined by a new model based on the same styling, the Mark VIII. Visually the Mark VIII brought the body style more up-to-date with a chromium-plated swage line running along the whole length of the body following the wing line. This gave the impression of less height and was accompanied in a majority of cases by new two-tone paint finishes, the chromium stripe forming the 'break' between one colour and the other, an effect which pandered to North American tastes. There were still rear spats although they accommodated a cut-away to reveal more of the wheel.

Two significant changes concerned the windscreen and radiator grille. The former now became a one-piece curved screen while the latter, although of similar slat design, received a pronounced Mark V style chromium-plated surround. In addition a chromium-plated leaping Jaguar mascot was fitted on the leading edge of the bonnet.

Mechanically the XK engine as fitted to the Mark VIII came with the latest 'B' type cylinder head with larger valves, new inlet manifold, twin pipe exhaust system and the later type SU carburettors, all of which provided welcome extra torque for the big saloon. Another advance was made in the automatic transmission with the fitment of a special intermediate Speed

Hold switch which, when operated, kept the transmission in its intermediate gear and prevented the 'box from changing up and down needlessly under spirited driving. A few Mark VIIIs were also fitted with a power steering system intended as a standard equipment item for the later Mark IX.

Even more improvements were to be found on the inside of the Mark VIII. All cars (whether fitted with individual or bench type front seats) now featured wood veneer fold-away picnic tables for the rear seat passengers. On bench seat cars there was an electric clock and a magazine rack, again finished in veneer. The rear seat itself was reshaped to resemble individual seating and it was also better cushioned.

The air of heightened luxury continued with other minor trim improvements including the fitment of no less than three cigarette lighters! Even the boot received attention with the installation of Hardura matting for the whole area including the spare wheel cover.

The Mark VIII lasted in production for only a little over three years, by which time it had been superseded by a yet further improved model, the Mark IX.

MARK IX

October 1958 saw the launch of the next variation on the Mark VII theme, the Mark IX. Initially it was built alongside the Mark VIII and the two models were actually featured side-by-side in certain company brochures.

Externally it was impossible to tell the difference between a Mark VIII and a Mark IX except for the discreet badging on the boot lid. Internally, minor changes to the calibration of the rev counter, a rear compartment magazine rack and a couple of switches were the only distinguishing features.

Under the bonnet, however, it was a different story. The capacity of the XK engine had been increased to 3.8 litres (3781cc) necessitating the use of a new block with liners yet retaining the 'B' type cylinder head. The result was an increase in power to 220bhp and an increase of over 11 per cent in torque.

Extra brightwork on the Mark VIII had the effect of making it look less tall. With yet more torque available, it was also more comfortable to drive. Interior was improved, particularly for rear passengers. Note the gear selector for the automatic gearbox sited above the steering column; it had a 'speed hold' function for spirited driving.

The last of the separate chassis Jaguars, the Mark IX lasted until 1961, having firmly established Jaguar as perhaps the world's leading luxury saloon car maker at that time. Apart from badging, it was externally indistinguishable from the MkVIII. Rear passengers benefited from veneered picnic tables and a magazine rack.

To cope with the increased performance the Mark IX also benefited from four-wheel disc brakes by Dunlop with a Lockheed servo, while all Mark IXs were fitted with Burman power-assisted steering. The end result of these mechanical changes was a more modern and practical motorcar still able to set the pace against its competitors.

With many minor modifications over the following years, the Mark IX continued in production until 1961 when it was replaced by a brand new large Jaguar saloon for the 1960s.

MARK VIIIB

The story of the Mark VII to IX cars does not end here, however. A limited number of the so-called Mark VIIIB model was produced based around the Mark VIII and IX. All were

destined for special roles within the military, the government – or even as hearses. Externally a Mark VIIIB looked like any other example but featured a low compression engine, usually manual transmission (although with a bench front seat) and limousine style fitments such as a glass division. Some cars were even fitted with flag mountings on the bonnet. Most of these cars were painted black. Recorded deliveries actually continued until after the production of the Mark IX had ceased.

Total production of all Mark VII bodied cars amounted to some 47,000 units spread over eleven years. In that time the models built up a strong following and set the standards by which other large luxury cars were judged. The Mark IX was the last separate chassis Jaguar ever made.

The Mark IX's expanded 3.8-litre 220bhp XK engine (above) certainly made itself felt on the road. Mark VIIIB was the name given to certain special Mark VIIIs intended for carriage trade roles. This enormous hearse conversion (below) has a greatly lengthened tail section.

SPECIFICATIONS

MARK VII (1950-54)
Engine: 3442cc six-cylinder twin overhead camshaft
Bore & stroke: 83 × 106mm
Power output: 160bhp at 5200rpm
Transmission: Four-speed manual (later with Laycock de Normanville overdrive on top gear) or Borg Warner three-speed automatic
Wheelbase: 10ft (305cm)
Length: 16ft 4½in (499cm)
Width: 6ft 1in (185cm)
Height: 5ft 3in (160cm)
Weight: 34½cwt (1753kg)
Suspension: Front: independent, wishbone, torsion bar, anti-roll bar. Rear: live axle, half elliptic leaf springs
Brakes: Girling hydraulic servo assisted
Top speed: 100mph (160kmh)
0-50mph (80kmh): 9.8 secs
Price new: £1276

MARK VIIM (1954-57)
As Mark VII except:
Power output: 190bhp at 5500rpm
Transmission: Four-speed manual with Laycock de Normanville overdrive on top gear or Borg Warner three-speed automatic
Weight: 34¾cwt (1765kg)

Top speed: 105mph (168kmh)
Price new: £1616
Total Mark VII Production: Mark VII 20,939; Mark VIIM 9261 **Grand Total** 30,200

MARK VIII (1956-59)
As Mark VII except:
Power output: 210bhp at 5500rpm
Weight: 34¾cwt (1765kg)
Top speed: 106mph (170kmh)
0-50mph (80kmh): 8.7 secs
Price new: £1830
Total Mark VIII Production: 6332

MARK IX (1958-61)
As Mark VII except:
Engine: 3781cc six-cylinder twin overhead camshaft
Bore & stroke: 87 × 106mm
Power output: 220bhp at 5500rpm
Weight: 35½cwt (1803kg)
Brakes: Dunlop four-wheel discs, servo-assisted
Top speed: 115mph (184kmh)
0-50mph (80kmh): 8.5 secs
Price new: £1994
Total Mark IX Production: 10,005

CHAPTER EIGHT

XK140

1954-57

The XK140 model most altered as against the XK120 was the Fixed Head Coupé. To accommodate an extra pair of rear seat passengers, the roof was lengthened, rather spoiling the aesthetics of the coupé for the sake of practicality.

The XK140 was very much a development of the original XK120 concept with greater emphasis placed on practicality and comfort. Originally Jaguar had intended to launch an entirely new sports car to replace the XK120, and this is probably why there was a model jump from this designation to XK140 leaving out the '130'. Due to severe pressures on production facilities and the lack of development time, Jaguar decided instead to upgrade the XK rather than replace it; thus the XK140 was born.

The new model was launched at the British Motor Show at Earls Court in 1954 and from the outset was available in all body styles: Roadster, Drophead Coupé and Fixed Head Coupé. Mechanically similar in most respects to the previous model, the standard XK140 now boasted 190bhp from its XK SE-type engine with ⅜in lift camshafts and single exhaust system. The C-type cylinder head was available as a cost option; in this form the engine developed 210bhp.

Other mechanical changes included a more efficient cooling system with inclined radiator, eight-blade cooling fan and Alford & Alder rack-and-pinion steering, while Laycock de Normanville overdrive was also available to aid the XK's cruising ability. Suspension was basically the same as in the XK120 except for uprated front springs and Girling telescopic shock absorbers replacing the old lever arm type. Brakes were also carried over from the XK120 except for the fitment of a single master cylinder. The batteries were repositioned in the front wings.

Resiting the engine 3in further forward in the chassis allowed the bulkhead to move forward as well, providing additional space inside the car. The extra room made possible the fitment of two occasional rear seats and a more inclined steering wheel position.

The bodywork of the XK140 was basically unchanged over the earlier cars although the new model lost some of its 'cleanness' with the fitment of much heavier chrome adornments like the centre bonnet and boot trims, cast radiator grille and substantial Mark VII style bumpers with overriders. The bumpers increased the length of the XK by three inches. The

An extra two seats certainly made the XK140 Fixed Head (above) more usable but it was no longer such a pretty car. The Drophead Coupé version (below) combined the best elements of the Roadster and Fixed Head models, while still managing to look shapely and dignified with hood up or down.

new XKs also featured 'J' type headlights, matching fog and spot lights on the front bumper valance and wing-mounted indicators. New 16in steel or wire wheels (at extra cost) were offered for the XK140.

All models proudly boasted Jaguar's Le Mans success on a plaque mounted on the boot lid next to the push-button boot lock and handle. The Drophead and Fixed Head models had the luxury of push-button external door handles.

The ultra-civilised Fixed Head Coupé now provided a much more airy interior with increased window areas, wider doors and 1½in more headroom. Walnut veneer was retained for both this model and the Drophead Coupé. Despite having a convertible roof, the

Drophead still accommodated the same new rear seating arrangement as the Fixed Head. The Roadster carried forward the XK tradition of a vinyl covered dashboard (although the angle of the dash was now completely vertical) and this model also featured aluminium door panels.

Prices for the XK140s were still very competitive, from as little as £1598 for the Roadster and £1830 for the other variants. The XK140 was something of a stop-gap model to maintain customer interest in the XK during the mid-1950s while a more substantially revised version was prepared. A total of only 9051 XK140s were made up to the end of production in February 1957.

Rear seats of sorts in the DHC (above): really suitable for children only, but a useful advance over the XK120. This Roadster (below) shows clearly the XK140's revised front end: thicker bumpers, more brightwork and a cast radiator grille. Wire wheels became an increasingly popular option, in which case the rear wheel spats had to be removed to accommodate the spinners.

SPECIFICATIONS

XK140 (1954-57)

Engine: 3442cc six-cylinder twin overhead camshaft
Bore & stroke: 83 × 106mm
Power output: 190bhp at 5500rpm (standard)/210bhp at 5750rpm (Special Equipment)
Transmission: Manual four-speed with or without overdrive, or three-speed automatic
Wheelbase: 8ft 6in (259cm)
Length: 14ft 8in (447cm)
Width: 5ft 4½in (164cm)

Height: 4ft 4½in (133cm)
Weight: 28cwt (1422kg)
Suspension: Front: independent, wishbone, torsion bars, anti-roll bar. Rear: live axle, half elliptic leaf springs
Brakes: Lockheed hydraulic drums
Top speed: 121mph (194kmh)
0-50mph (80kmh): 6.5 secs
Price new: £1598
Total Production: Roadster 3354; Fixed Head 2808; Drophead 2889 **Grand Total 9051**

CHAPTER NINE

XK150

1957-61

The straight-through wing line of the XK150 looks best on the Drophead and Roadster models, and this view shows the widened front grille, reshaped bonnet and leaping cat mascot. This Drophead features body-coloured wire wheels, a standard option when new.

Although the XK140 officially ceased production in February 1957, its replacement the XK150 was not actually announced until May of that year. The XK150 was to prove the final development on the XK theme. It was released initially only in Drophead or Fixed Head Coupé body styles, the Roadster version only becoming available in 1958 and then initially for the export trade alone.

On the mechanical side the big news for the XK150 was the standard fitment of Dunlop 12in disc brakes on all four wheels plus power assistance. The chassis, steering and suspension were carried over from the previous model except for the fitment of Nyloc interleafing in the springs and rubber mountings between the rack-and-pinion steering and the chassis.

Mechanically the standard XK150 3.4-litre engine was the same as before, developing 190bhp, or 210bhp with the B-type cylinder head and larger exhaust valves developed from the C-type. A modified manifold with separate water jacket and twin SU HD6 1¾in carburettors were also fitted to this 'Special Equipment' engine.

Bodily the XK style was substantially updated, yet it retained the typical Jaguar sports car look. A wider slatted radiator grille, a more slab-sided appearance due to the raising of the body feature line, a full wraparound rear bumper and higher scuttle all helped to make the car look heavier and bulkier than the earlier

The Roadster also received the new side contour treatment but still retained curved door tops. A tonneau somehow suits the Roadster better than the hood.

XKs. The use of a semi-wrap-around one piece windscreen was also new for Jaguar, replacing the old split-screen type on previous XKs. Another first for Jaguar was the fitment of the leaping cat mascot to the bonnet top of an XK sports car.

Inside, the new XK150 became the most civilised Jaguar sports car yet, boasting more room, softer and wider seating and – a first for an XK – a padded

Leather for the facia, a dashtop roll and more comfortable seating were the main advances in the XK150's interior.

vinyl covered dashboard featuring revised instrumentation. For the first time too, an XK Roadster featured wind-up glass windows with chromium-plated surrounds and even a chrome finisher to the top of the slightly curved door tops. The Fixed Head boasted even more window area and American-style sliding door release levers. All this added up to a heavier car and the Fixed head Coupé weighed in at around 29cwt, a full 1cwt heavier than the equivalent XK140 model.

The prettiest of the XK150 models was undoubtedly the Roadster, released in March 1958, which

recalled the style of the original XK120 of 1948. There were no rear occasional seats and the rear bodywork was carried forward to meet the back of the front seats, leaving just enough room for the Mohair hood to fold away out of sight, so the roadster looked longer, lower and sleeker than its two sister models.

With the three different body styles running concurrently, Jaguar introduced a further option in the form of the XK150S. The new 'S' engine featured re-designed Weslake cylinder heads (later known as straight-port), three 2in SU carburettors, new manifolding, lead bronze bearings, stronger clutch, lighter flywheel and a standardised compression ratio of 9:1. The new 'S' engine was rated at 250bhp at 5500rpm and, at the same time as these engines started to appear in XK150s, the disc braking system came in for revision with the introduction of square quick-change pads developed from the D-type.

By 1960 the XK150 model range had expanded still further with the availability of the 3.8-litre (3781cc)

Delightful period shot of the XK150 Roadster (above) reveals its more up-to-date lines and increasingly practical features. Proper wind-up windows and a hood which looked less like an afterthought made this the most practical XK Roadster yet (below).

engine as well (first seen in the Mark IX saloon two years earlier). The 3.8-litre XK150 came either in the standard B-type twin carburettor tune or in 'S' specification with triple carburettors, in which form it developed a handsome 265bhp. At just under £2200 it was exceptional value for money and ideally suited to the lucrative North American market where, increasingly, a very high level of performance was expected from a sports car.

The XK150 remained in production until 1961 by which time just under 9400 had been produced of all models. The last of the traditional chassis sporting Jaguars gave way to a brand new sports car for the future – the E-type.

The glass area of the Fixed Head was again enhanced (above). Like all XK150s, it had a new one-piece curved windscreen. There was a lot more elbow room in an XK150 (below) thanks to slimmer doors. Because the seat backs were thinner, rear seat passengers also gained more legroom.

SPECIFICATIONS

XK150 (1957-61)

Engine: 3442cc/3781cc six-cylinder twin overhead camshaft
Bore & stroke: 83 × 106mm/87mm × 106mm
Power output: 190bhp at 5500rpm (3.4-litre standard); 210bhp at 5500rpm (3.4-litre Special Equipment); 250bhp at 5500rpm (3.4-litre S); 220bhp at 5500rpm (3.8-litre standard); 265bhp at 5500rpm (3.8-litre S)
Transmission: Four-speed manual, optional overdrive
Wheelbase: 8ft 6in (259cm)
Length: 14ft 9in (450cm)
Width: 5ft 4½in (164cm)
Height: 4ft 6in (137cm)
Weight: 28½cwt (1448kg)/29cwt (1473kg) FHC

Suspension: Front: independent, wishbone, torsion bar, anti-roll bar. Rear: live axle, semi-elliptic leaf springs
Brakes: Dunlop discs, hydraulic vacuum servo
Top speed: 132mph (211kmh) 3.4-litre; 136mph (218kmh) 3.4-litre S; 134mph (215kmh) 3.8-litre; 138mph (221kmh) 3.8-litre S
0-50mph (80kmh): 6.1 secs (3.4-litre); 5.6 secs (3.4-litre S); 5.8 secs (3.8-litre); 5.4 secs (3.8-litre S)
Price new: £1763 to £2175
Total Production:
Roadster 3.4 1297, 3.4S 888, 3.8 42, 3.8S 36; Fixed Head 3.4 3445, 3.4S 199, 3.8 656, 3.8S 150; Drophead 3.4 1903, 3.4S 104, 3.8 586, 3.8S 89 **Grand Total** 9395

MARK 1 & 2, INCLUDING 240/340

1956-69

2.4-LITRE (1956-59)

Up to 1956 Jaguar had consistently followed a one-model policy in respect of its saloons but, after the successful introduction of the Mark VII, it realised the potential expansion of its market and the advantage of diminishing overheads which the development of a smaller saloon range might offer. By utilising as many parts as possible from the Mark VII and XK140 sports car, the cost of production could be much reduced.

So in 1956, after £100,000 worth of development, Jaguar launched its first compact saloon, the 2.4-Litre (later referred to as the Mark 1, after the introduction of its successor, the Mark 2). Advanced for its period and certainly over-engineered, the car was a first for Jaguar in having a chassis-less monocoque construction. The body was built up of two main longitudinal box sections running fore to aft and welded to the ribbed steel floorpan. Transverse members linked these throughout the length of the body, the whole structure held even tauter by the front scuttle and rear seat-pan. Two additional box members ran either side from the front end up to the bulkhead for further strength.

All outer panels were made of steel and welded into place, including the sills which themselves formed strong box sections. As a result the bodyshell was immensely rigid, additionally benefiting from heavy screen pillars, a relatively small back window area and doors with integral steel window frames.

Stylistically the 2.4 subtly developed the 'family look' of the 1950s Jaguars, with dominant XK-style frontal themes, a cast XK140-type grille, matching fog/spot lights and a ribbed bumper. At the rear the parallels with the sports car continued, with a swept down boot and more brightwork around the number-plate mount. In profile the new 2.4 saloon looked vastly more smooth and modern than the Mark VII, and in some respects it looked even more substantial thanks to a reduction in chrome adornment around the window surrounds. The 2.4 was never offered in any two-tone paint finishes from the factory due to the absence of any swage lining. Full spats covered the rear wheels, providing another strong echo of the Mark VII.

At first it was intended to use a four-cylinder engine in the compact car but Sir William Lyons wanted smoothness, besides which there was a strong need to utilise parts from the existing Jaguar range. This meant the development of a brand new configuration of the well-tried XK six-cylinder engine already used in all other Jaguars. The 'new' engine was of 2483cc, retaining the existing bore yet having a shorter stroke of only 76.5mm (compared to 106mm in the 3.4-litre version). Therefore the block was more

At its launch in 1956, the Mark 1 was a revelation for Jaguar: a smaller luxury car with full-width bodywork and modern styling. Full spats covered the rear wheels on all Mark 1s with steel wheels.

Another first for Jaguar: chassis-less all-new monocoque construction. The 2.4-litre engine was a de-stroked six-cylinder XK unit and the whole car was arguably over-engineered. The rear track was 4¼in narrower than the front.

The 3.4-litre XK engine provided the Mark 1 with a remarkable turn of speed for its day. When the optional wire wheels were specified, cut-away spats were fitted.

compact, which meant a welcome weight saving of around 50lbs. The twin overhead camshaft layout was retained, with engine breathing restricted by the use of twin downdraught Solex B32 carburettors and ⁵⁄₁₆in lift cams.

The 2.4-litre unit was rated at 112bhp at 5750rpm and drove through a single dry plate Borg and Beck clutch and conventional four-speed gearbox, available with or without Laycock de Normanville overdrive and connected to a Salisbury 3HA differential.

For the suspension Jaguar chose a coil spring set-up at the front, with twin rear inclined wishbones of unequal length, the coils attached to the lower wishbones and retained by hollow steel pillars on which the top wishbones pivoted. Conventional upper and lower ball joints were used to accommodate wheel movement and steering. Girling telescopic shock absorbers were secured inside the coil springs, acting on the bottom wishbone and anchored at the top. An anti-roll bar was also fitted.

The curvaceous line of the 1956 2.4-Litre (later dubbed the Mark 1) were distinctively Jaguar and could be traced in other Jaguar saloons until the late 1960s. Compare the wider radiator grille of the 1957 3.4-Litre Mark 1 (below) with the early 2.4; this treatment would also be adopted by the later 2.4. Body-coloured wire wheels made the 3.4-Litre look more sporting.

Burman recirculating steering was used on the 2.4 and a separate front subframe carrying the suspension and steering was detachable from the car as a complete unit, the subframe being isolated from the car by rubber blocks to ensure effective absorption of noise and road shocks.

At the rear, a cart spring layout was adopted although the conventional five leaf springs were turned upside down and anchored to the car at their front end inside the rear chassis rails. The cantilevered rear axle was located by twin trailing arms running from the seat pan area to brackets above the axle, and an adjustable Panhard rod was used for side location. Girling telescopic shock absorbers were again used at the rear located through the wheelarch to the rear boot area via rubber mountings.

Interestingly the 2.4 had a very obviously narrower rear track of only 4ft 2¼in compared to 4ft 6½in at the front. The fitment of the full depth spats helped to disguise this unattractive feature.

The new car rode on Dunlop 6.40 × 15 tyres fitted to steel rims accommodating the traditional Jaguar hubcaps. Lockheed drum brakes with servo assistance were featured on all four wheels.

Although compact by Jaguar's standards (the 2.4 was exactly 15ft long, some 15 inches shorter than the Mark VII), the new car suffered no compromises in internal luxury. In Special Equipment form, the 2.4 came with Vaumol leather faced seating, walnut veneer dashboard and window frame surrounds, two front bucket seats and a three-abreast bench at the rear, plus a comprehensive array of instrumentation and fitments. The S.E. model was released at the attractive price of only £1298.

Alongside the Special Equipment model Jaguar also catalogued (although it is not known exactly how many were made) a Standard model, which came without a heater/demister, rev counter or folding centre armrest in the rear bench seat, without screen washers, fog/spot lights, cigar lighter, courtesy light switch, leaping cat mascot or enamelled exhaust manifolds. Listed at £1269, the Standard model was self-evidently a poor choice when compared with the better-equipped S.E. version at only £30 dearer!

3.4-LITRE (1957-59)

With the success of the 2.4-Litre saloon Jaguar was keen to exploit the model's potential, and in February 1957 it introduced a 3.4-litre engined version utilising the XK140 3442 cc six-cylinder engine with twin HD6 SU carburettors, producing some 210bhp. Despite the horrendous factory fire of that month the new model started to arrive in the showrooms by March priced at just under £1700.

No compromise on luxury in Jaguar's compact saloon. Manual transmission cars generally had separate bucket seats, while automatics had a split bench front seat.

Very little needed to be modified to accommodate the more powerful engine in the existing bodyshell. The radiator grille was widened, with narrower slats (a feature which was later to find its way on to the 2.4-Litre), and there was a larger radiator, a twin exhaust system, improved engine mountings, a 1in larger diameter clutch, a revised gearbox mounting, a Salisbury 4HA differential, an amended Panhard rod mounting and some other minor detail changes. The only other external changes were the fitment of '3.4' badging and cut-down rear wheel spats to aid brake cooling.

Automatic transmission became available on the 3.4, and later on the 2.4-Litre as well, and was operated by means of a dashboard mounted quadrant, allowing the fitment of split bench-type seating at the front.

Virtually immediately after the launch of the 3.4, Jaguar introduced disc brakes on all four wheels for both models, after which both cars continued in production without significant change until the end of 1959, by which time a total of just under 20,000 2.4s and 17,405 3.4s had been made. These figures represented a significant boost to Jaguar's production.

The compact saloons were also to find favour on the competition front in both rallying and saloon car racing, as well as for the private use of many celebrated professional drivers who appreciated the superb performance qualities of the Jaguar.

THE MARK 2 (1959-67)

The 2.4- and 3.4-Litre compact saloons only became known as Mark 1s after the introduction of Jaguar's updated Mark 2 at the Motor Show in 1959. Based on the well-received Mark 1 principles, the new car marked a significant advance on the compact formula, creating quite a storm in 1959.

The Mark 2 signified a major move forward in styling, with slimmed-down separate chromed window frames and a larger rear window for a much brighter interior, a redesigned cabin, a rear track widened by 3¼in and generally more brightwork.

The launch of the Mark 2 in 1959 created as much of a stir as that of the Mark 1. Here was unequivocally one of the best saloon cars made in the world.

Overall the effect was to modernise the Mark 1 shape.

Distinguishing features included a new radiator grille (now sporting a thick central bar incorporating the engine size badge), new style flush-fitting fog/spot lights, circular indicators, chromed rain gutters to the roof, slimmer door handles and chrome-on-brass window frames (styled like those of the Mark IX).

Internally the new model benefited from a total restyle featuring larger front bucket seats (now with flush fitting picnic tables in their backs). A totally redesigned dashboard set the trend for other Jaguar saloons and sports cars of the 1960s, siting the speedometer and rev counter in front of the driver with ancillary gauges and switches on a centrally mounted panel. A centre console running down from the dashboard incorporated controls for the uprated 3.9 kilowatt heater, a radio and speaker, the gearlever and heating ducts to the rear compartment. Traditional Jaguar touches were not forgotten: indeed the use of leather and walnut veneer reached new levels of opulence.

Mechanically the big news for the Mark 2 was the availability of all three configurations of the XK six-cylinder engine: the existing 2.4-litre with Solex carburation, the existing 3.4-litre with twin SUs and then the top-of-the-range 3.8-litre twin SU engine developing 220bhp (taken directly from the Mark IX). Existing gearboxes were carried over, providing a choice of automatic transmission or a four-speed manual 'box with or without overdrive. There were other minor mechanical modifications but in the main the successful package was carried over directly from the Mark 1.

The 2.4-litre version was still the slowest of the range and in fact, due to extra weight of the Mark 2 bodyshell, it was slightly slower than the earlier model with a 0-50mph time of 12.7 seconds (11 seconds for the Mark 1). The 3.8-litre, however, could really motor along, reaching 50mph in only 6.4 seconds and boasting a maximum speed of over 125mph.

A modest £1534 would buy you a 2.4-litre Mark 2 in 1959 while, for the 3.8-litre model (then the fastest production saloon car in the world), you still needed to pay only £1800.

The Mark 2 models were updated throughout an

illustrious lifespan. Perhaps the most important changes came in September 1965, when all models received the new Jaguar four-speed all-synchromesh gearbox which had been fitted on the Mark X and E-type twelve months earlier. With it came a new, more efficient diaphragm spring clutch.

Another major change came in September 1966 when Jaguar sales generally were beginning to decline, necessitating a more economical approach to production. In the case of the Mark 2 this meant the standard fitment of Ambla (plastic) upholstery instead of leather (although this could still be ordered as an option at extra cost) and the deletion of the paired fog/spot lights, replaced by chromium-plated grilles.

As a last fling, in 1967 Jaguar decided to make available the new Marles Varamatic power steering system on Mark 2s. But by then economic pressures forced further cost cut-backs, and these led to a change in model designation.

The 1959 Mark 2 (above) had a much larger glass area than the Mark 1 and chrome window surrounds. All Mark 2s (there were 2.4, 3.4 and 3.8-litre versions) had cut-away rear spats to accommodate the wider rear track. The celebrated Mark 2 record breaker (below) on the track at Monza during its endurance record run. Note the roof-mounted wiper.

240/340 (1967-69)

By 1967 Jaguar was starting to rationalise its saloon car range, ultimately returning to a one-model policy with the introduction of the XJ6. This meant the demise of the 3.8-litre Mark 2 in September 1967 and the re-designation of the 2.4 and 3.4-litre Mark 2s as the 240 and 340 respectively.

With the model name change came other reductions in specification, notably the fitment of S-type slimline front and rear bumper bars (which necessitated re-styled valances) and new hub caps.

Mechanical changes were for the better, notably the introduction of the straight-port cylinder head which improved performance of the 2.4-litre engine significantly, and which was aided by the fitment of twin HS6 SU carburettors and a standard-type air cleaner. Power went up to 133bhp at 5500rpm and with it acceleration moved up a couple more notches: 0 to 50mph was achieved in 9.3 seconds. The 340 – also with a straight-port cylinder head – was blessed with an improvement in performance to not far behind the 3.8's, at 6.9 seconds to 50mph and a top speed of 124mph.

At a launch price of £1365 the 240 represented excellent value for money when compared with the original 2.4-litre Mark 2 of 1959, which had a very similar price. The 340 was similarly competitively priced at £1442.

The 340 was to remain in production only until September 1968 with a relatively small production run of 2796, the 240 soldiering on to April 1969 with a slighter larger production total of 4446.

The compact Jaguar saloons hold a special place in the history of the marque as they proved to be the most popular of all models up to the introduction of the XJ6 and satisfied the needs of so many different types of owners, from the private sector to the racing and rally fraternity. The Mark 1 and 2 proved competitive in the hands of drivers like Mike Hawthorn, Duncan Hamilton, Ivor Bueb and Roy Salvadori.

A grand total of over 128,000 of these compact saloons were produced from 1956 to 1969, a tribute to the excellence of the design and to Jaguar's marketing strategy at the time.

From the front (above), the Mark 2 was recognisable by the centre bar on its radiator grille and different side, indicator and fog lights. The 3.8-litre Mark 2 (below left) was the most powerful version and was comfortably the world's fastest production saloon in the early 1960s. Larger Mark 2 rear window (below right) is visible in this shot of a 3.4-litre version with chrome wire wheels.

The traditionally luxurious Jaguar treatment made the Mark 2 a car in which drivers of larger saloons would feel happy and a compact car to which other drivers could aspire.

Although the XK engine looked a tight fit in the Mark 2 bay, most components were easily accessible. This is a later example with unpolished ribbed camshaft covers.

The 240 and 340 were identifiable by their slimmer bumpers, making the rear valance panel look larger. Although the 340 was stripped of some of its equipment in Jaguar's 1967 rationalisation, this example (above) is fully equipped with optional fog lamps, wire wheels and leather upholstery.

SPECIFICATIONS

2.4/3.4-LITRE MARK 1 (1956-59)
Engine: 2483cc/3442cc six-cylinder twin overhead camshaft
Bore & stroke: 83 × 76.5mm/83mm × 106mm
Power output: 112bhp at 5750rpm/210bhp at 5500rpm
Transmission: Four-speed manual with or without over-drive, or Borg Warner three-speed automatic
Wheelbase: 8ft 11½in (273cm)
Length: 15ft (457cm)
Width: 5ft 6½in (169cm)
Height: 4ft 9½in (146cm)
Weight: 27/28½cwt (1372/1448kg)
Suspension: Front: independent, semi-trailing double wishbones, coil springs, anti-roll bar. Rear: cantilevered live axle, radius arms, Panhard rod, half elliptic leaf springs
Brakes: Lockheed Brakemaster hydraulic drums, vacuum assisted (later Dunlop four-wheel discs with vacuum assistance)
Top speed: 101/120mph (162/192kmh)
0-50mph (80kmh): 11 secs/7 secs
Price new: £1344/£1672
Total Production: 2.4-Litre 19,992; 3.4-Litre 17,405 **Grand Total** 37,397

2.4/3.4/3.8-LITRE MARK 2 (1959-67)
As for Mark 1 except:
Engine: 2483cc/3442cc/3781cc six-cylinder twin overhead camshaft
Bore & stroke: 83 × 76.5mm/83mm × 106mm/87mm × 106mm

Power output: 120bhp at 5750rpm/210bhp at 5500rpm/220bhp at 5500rpm
Weight: 28½/29½cwt (1448/1499kg)
Suspension: Front: independent, double wishbones, coil springs, anti-roll bar
Brakes: Dunlop four-wheel discs with vacuum assistance
Top speed: 96/120/125mph (154/192/200kmh)
0-50mph (80kmh): 12.7 secs/9 secs/6.4 secs
Price new: £1534/£1669/£1779
Total Production: Mark 2 2.4-litre 25,173; Mark 2 3.4-litre 28,666; Mark 2 3.8-litre 30,141 **Grand Total** 83,980

240 (1967-69)
As Mark 2 2.4-litre except:
Power output: 133bhp at 5500rpm
Length: 14ft 11in (455cm)
Top speed: 106mph (170kmh)
0-50mph (80kmh): 9.3 secs
Price New: £1365
Total Production: 4446

340 (1967-68)
As Mark 2 3.4-litre except:
Length: 14ft 11in (455cm)
Weight: 30cwt (1524kg)
Top speed: 124mph (198kmh)
0-50mph (80kmh): 6.9 secs
Price new: £1442
Total Production: 2796

DAIMLER 2.5-LITRE V8

1956-69

SP250 (1959-64)

The Daimler SP250 (*aka* Dart) sports car would not fall within the aegis of this book except for the fact that, when Jaguar purchased the Daimler company in 1960, it was one of the inherited designs that was to continue in production for some time after the take-over. The name Dart which had been originally intended for the model was withdrawn due to a conflict with the American Dodge company which also used the name for one of its sporting saloons. The Daimler was therefore re-designated the SP250, a model number that remained with the car until its demise.

By far the best aspect of the take-over for Jaguar was the acquisition of important manufacturing facilities at the Daimler Radford factory in nearby Coventry as well as the extremely reputable and valued name of Daimler, a marque which Sir William Lyons was determined to keep alive. As far as the cars were concerned, the fine 2547cc V8 engine, designed by Edward Turner, that powered the Daimler SP250 was of particular in-

terest. This extremely well-designed and compact engine made extensive use of aluminium and was incredibly smooth and quiet in operation, developing around 140bhp.

A 90 degree cast iron block with twin interchangeable aluminium cylinder heads had pushrod operated valves with its camshaft mounted high in the centre of the block. With twin SU carburettors, the V8 engine was very free-revving and performed well through a conventional four-speed manual gearbox.

The engine was developed especially for the Daimler designed SP250, and the car was a complete breakaway for the traditionally-minded Daimler company in offering rather avant garde styling and a bodyshell made completely of glassfibre, albeit on a conventional chassis. Some recognisable Daimler styling motifs and the familiar fluted radiator grille identified the car as a Daimler, although generally speaking the rather extravagant styling was reminiscent of some of the plastic bodyshells produced by specials manufacturers in the 1950s. Strictly a two-seater of similar proportions

Unconventional in both styling and glassfibre construction, the SP250's bodywork perhaps explained customer resistance. However, the SP250 certainly performed well, its V8 engine matching the sporting character of Jaguar's own XK.

This denuded left-hand drive SP250 shows the simple separate chassis and the splendid 2.5-litre aluminium V8 engine designed by Edward Turner, which could take the one-ton SP250 to 124mph.

to the contemporary MGA, the SP250 offered leather upholstery and the usual trappings associated with an upmarket sports car, including wind-up glass windows, still a relative rarity at that time.

It was released with high hopes in 1959 and, whilst its 120mph top speed and good acceleration should have helped sell the car, sales were disappointing, probably due to the outlandish styling and the fact that many highly advanced sports cars were coming on the scene, not least of which was the E-type Jaguar in 1961.

Jaguar made a couple of attempts to re-design the car to produce something a little more acceptable, and even David Ogle produced an extremely attractive alternative, which in due course found its way to Reliant to become the first Scimitar.

Jaguar eventually decided to drop the SP250 from production in 1964 as it was judged superfluous alongside its own E-type, of which not enough were being produced to satisfy demand. Despite its chequered life, the SP250 today is a much sought-after classic. After the event, its individual styling and superb mechanicals are easier to appreciate.

Befitting a sports car within a range of luxury cars, the Daimler was well-appointed inside, with leather and, unusually, wind-up windows.

2.5-LITRE V8 SALOON (1962-66)

Jaguar's engineers soon realised the potential of the Daimler 2.5-litre V8 engine and, after successful testing in a Mark 1 bodyshell, they set to work adapting the unit to fit the Mark 2 saloon. Very little alteration was needed other than revising the shape of the oil sump to accommodate the Jaguar's front cross-member and the use of bolts instead of studs to secure the heads in position so that they could be removed with the engine in situ. Also there were new exhaust manifolds and downpipes to create sufficient clearance in the engine bay, leading to twin exhaust pipes and silencers which emerged at either rear corner of the car below bumper level. The cooling fan was resited and had to be operated via a belt from a new double grooved pulley, the second groove taking a belt from the pulley to the dynamo situated above.

The engine was fitted with twin 1¾in SU carburet-

tors with revised air cleaners. Because the Daimler engine was significantly lighter than Jaguar's own XK unit, the front spring rates were adapted accordingly and all cars were fitted as standard with power-assisted steering. The Daimler engine propelled the car through a standard Borg Warner Type 35 automatic transmission with no manual option available at that time. Interestingly none of the Daimler models was ever fitted with the famed automatic speed hold, a common feature on all Jaguar automatic saloons.

The new 'Daimlerised' version of the Mark 2 saloon significantly out-performed Jaguar's own 2.4-litre model, having a 0-60mph time of only 13.8 seconds (a whole two seconds quicker than the Jaguar), and also a top speed of 110mph.

In appearance the Daimler was differentiated from its Jaguar counterparts by the fitment of the traditional fluted radiator grille and rear boot plinth, a swept Daimler 'D' on the bonnet with more prominent bonnet centre chrome, 'D' features to the hub cap centres and, of course, Daimler badging on the rear of the car.

Internally, the 2.5-Litre retained the Jaguar's dashboard layout but it featured split bench type seating at the front, which necessitated the fitment of a revised, smaller centre console incorporating the radio and heater controls with a separately mounted speaker underneath. Minor lighting changes were made for the Daimler and a bold 'D' naturally featured on the centre horn push of the steering wheel. Veneer quality was improved for the Daimler models, although for some reason rear picnic tables were never a feature of these cars.

The release of the Daimler 2.5-Litre V8 saloon in 1962 at around £100 dearer than the equivalent Jaguar saw the company clearly aiming the new car at a different segment of the market. Whereas the Jaguar was targeted more at sporting motorists, the Daimler tended to draw a more traditional and professional clientele.

A very small number of manual transmission models were made available during production; the adoption of such a gearbox improved performance.

Daimler introduced its extraordinary V8 SP250 sports car one year before Jaguar's take-over in 1960. It was a radical departure.

In the Mark 2 bodyshell, the V8 engine was capable of taking the car to 110mph, with all the torque and smoothness associated with V8s.

The first 'Daimlerised' Jaguar appeared in 1962, based on the 2.4-litre Mark 2. Called the 2.5-Litre V8, it had a fluted grille, Daimler badging, a revised interior and, of course, the V8 engine. The leaping Jaguar was replaced by a flying 'D' mascot.

V8 250 (1967-69)

At the same time that Jaguar decided to rationalise its saloon model range in 1967, so too the Daimler V8 came in for revision. In September 1967 the Daimler was redesignated V8 250 and adopted the new-look slimline bumper treatment and revised hub caps (although keeping the 'D' insignia). Unlike their Jaguar counterparts, all Daimlers retained their fog/spot lights and leather upholstery as standard equipment.

Other aspects of the interior were changed, including the fitment of a padded Ambla roll cover to the top of the dashboard, more modern seats with ventilated upholstery, and simplified wooden door cappings.

Mechanically the engine remained unchanged save for the fitment of separate air filters for each carburettor and the use of an alternator. As with the Jaguars, Varamatic power steering was now available on the Daimler and, for the first time, the Jaguar manual all-synchromesh gearbox (with or without overdrive) became a regular option to the more usual automatic transmission.

The launch price of the V8 250 was £1613 for the manual transmission car (plus £45 extra for the overdrive) and £1698 for the automatic model. The V8 continued in production until 1969 (a little longer than the equivalent Jaguar compact models), after which time the Turner-designed engine would never again be seen in a Daimler.

The compact V8 saloons established the value of a continued Daimler range within the Jaguar empire. However, these cars represented the only new models with a Daimler engine produced under the Jaguar regime, all future models being merely badge-engineered versions of Jaguar cars (except for the limited production DS420 limousine, which is described in the next chapter).

Modified and renamed V8 250 in 1967, the Daimler adopted slimmer bumpers, as on the Jaguar
240/340 models. Superior quality veneer (below) featured in a dash very similar to the Jaguar's.
Daimlers always had split bench front seating.

SPECIFICATIONS

SP250 SPORTS (1959-64)

Engine: 2548cc V8-cylinder overhead valve
Bore & stroke: 76 × 70mm
Power output: 140bhp at 5800rpm
Transmission: Four-speed manual
Wheelbase: 7ft 8in (234cm)
Length: 13ft 4½in (408cm)
Width: 5ft (152cm)
Height: 4ft 2½in (128cm)
Weight: 20cwt (1016kg)
Suspension: Front: independent, double wishbones, coil
springs. Rear: live axle, leaf springs, lever-type dampers
Brakes: Girling four-wheel discs
Top speed: 124mph (198kmh)
0-50mph (80kmh): 6.5 secs
Price new: £1355 **Total Production:** 2641

2.5-LITRE V8 (1962-66)

As SP250 Sports except:

Transmission: Four-speed manual with or without over-
drive or Borg Warner three-speed automatic
Wheelbase: 8ft 11½in (273cm)
Length: 15ft (457cm)
Width: 5ft 6½in (169cm)
Height: 4ft 9½in (146cm)
Weight: 29cwt (1473kg)
Suspension: Front: independent, double wishbones, coil
springs, anti-roll bar. Rear: cantilevered live axle, radius
arms, Panhard rod, half elliptic leaf springs
Brakes: Dunlop four-wheel discs, vacuum-assisted
Top speed: 110mph (176kmh)
0-50mph (80kmh): 9.6 secs
Price new: £1568 **Total Production:** 12,997

V8 250 (1967-69)

As 2.5-Litre V8 except:
Price new: £1613
Total Production: 4883

CHAPTER TWELVE

MAJESTIC MAJOR & DS420

1960-92

Jaguar inherited the new Daimler Majestic Major in 1960 and kept it in limited production for seven years. It found favour with those conservative customers who liked a powerful engine.

MAJESTIC MAJOR

Like the SP250 sports car covered in the last chapter, the Daimler Majestic saloons were another carryover from the Daimler company prior to the Jaguar takeover. Having had relative success with their 3.8-litre six-cylinder Daimler Majestic saloon in the latter half of the 1950s, Daimler opted to upgrade the car by fitting the much more refined and powerful Edward Turner-designed 4561cc V8 engine and renaming it the Majestic Major. The new model was released to the public in 1959.

Retaining the same, somewhat awkward body style as the previous Majestic with its rather bland rear wing treatment, the 220bhp V8 was much more able to cope with the 36cwt body and could propel the car

to 120mph, with suitably impressive acceleration times to match. In fact this was probably the fastest Daimler saloon produced up to that time and easily a match for other contemporary luxury cars.

Jaguar inherited the Majestic Major in 1960 with the takeover of Daimler and the model continued in very limited production up to 1967. Jaguar was so impressed with the V8 engine that one was later tested in a Mark X saloon bodyshell, in which it apparently achieved the impressive acceleration figure of 0-100mph in 30.9 seconds. However, Jaguar opted not to use the engine in its own products because it might have undermined its own XK power unit. At only around £400 dearer than the equivalent Jaguar Mark IX (and later Mark X), the Majestic Major offered a good alternative to the buyer who wanted more understated luxury than the brasher Jaguar.

Over the course of the 1960s, the Majestic Major was also available as a long-wheelbase limousine, designated DR450, with an extra two feet in overall length. This proved quite a popular model for the carriage trade, matching a healthy turn of speed and economy with exceptional passenger accommodation.

The Daimler models were gradually upgraded to include elements of Jaguar interior trim in an attempt to keep the cost of production down, as only around 15 cars per week were actually being built. The Daimler Majestic Major survived as the last truly traditional car from one of Britain's oldest marques and, whilst it never found favour with customers in large numbers, the model was certainly underestimated as it was something of a wolf in sheep's clothing. The Majestics slowly passed away in late 1967 without a fanfare and have since remained very much the 'sleeping princess' of the marque.

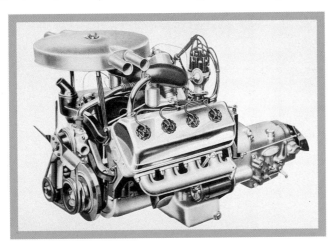

What made the Majestic Major special was its 4561cc 220bhp V8 engine, which could power this substantial car to around 120mph with ease.

DS420 (1968-92)

After the merger of Jaguar and Daimler with the British Motor Corporation in 1966, a corporate decision was taken to design and build a brand new limousine to replace the ageing Austin-based Vanden Plas Princess along with the Majestic Major DR450 from Daimler. Vanden Plas, which also formed part of the new British Motor Holdings Company, was chosen to design and build the body which, in fact, strongly resembled the Hooper Empress coachwork which had been fitted to many Daimler chassis.

To keep development costs down to a bare minimum, an existing engine and chassis had to be used and here the Jaguar 420G was the ideal donor. Jaguar supplied the bulkhead, wheelarches and floorpan to Motor Panels of Coventry who then extended the floorpan by 21in behind the centre door pillar and

added massive strengthening in the form of a transverse cross-member welded into the floor along with two 4in deep longitudinal box sections. The sills were dropped significantly to allow better ease of entry and exit from the rear compartment (a common problem on the Jaguar saloon) and massive deep sills were incorporated.

All exterior panelling was new, with extra steel welded into the front bulkhead to increase the overall height. The completed bodyshells were shipped to the Vanden Plas works in Kingsbury, London where full trimming and painting were carried out.

The Majestic Major's dashboard belonged more to the 1950s than the 1960s. A three-speed automatic gearbox was obligatory.

Mechanically the DS420 (as the new Daimler was to be known) utilised the six-cylinder 4.2-litre XK twin camshaft engine taken directly from the 420G but with only two SU carburettors and amended manifolding, reducing the output somewhat to around 177bhp. This was mated to a conventional Borg Warner automatic gearbox (manual was never available as an option). The only other mechanical changes over the 420G were revised springing and damper settings to compensate for the 42cwt body.

Internally the DS420 benefited from the specialised trimming skills of Vanden Plas, frequently to customers' own requirements, which included all manner of coverings from leather to dralon, moquette to West of England cloth. Rich veneer and quality carpeting were the norm, while standard equipment included a separate rear heater, generous lighting and occasional seating. On top of this any of the usual limousine trappings could be requested, from cocktail cabinets to electric centre divisions. At least one example was built as a mobile office incorporating fax, telephone, TV and computer. Landaulette versions were also offered with a folding hood at the rear.

Many standardised trim items were again taken

In long-wheelbase form (above) , the Majestic Major was known as the DR450 and was almost as popular as the standard-wheelbase version. Weighing two tons, it certainly needed that big V8 engine. At launch in 1968, Jaguar described the Daimler DS420 limousines (below) as having 'dignified styling'. Certainly its rear end harked back to pre-war days of swept wings and separate luggage boxes.

from the donor Jaguar 420G including instrumentation, switchgear and so on, while some of the very last cars produced also used items from the British Leyland parts bin. In 1980, after the demise of the Vanden Plas works, production was transferred to Jaguar's Browns Lane plant where a special department was set up with a small team of highly skilled labour to build the DS 420 by hand.

At 18ft 5in long, 5ft 2½in high and 6ft 4½in wide, the DS420 adequately fulfilled the needs of the carriage trade. Relatively inexpensive to purchase new compared to the alternatives from the likes of Rolls-Royce, moderately cheap to run and maintain due to the interchangeability of parts with Jaguars, yet carrying a certain aristocratic presence, the DS420 attracted the custom of wedding hire firms, mayors and funeral directors alike.

The very last DS420 limousine left the Jaguar factory late in 1992 after a total of 4116 complete cars

had been made, plus a further 927 supplied in chassis form to specialist coachbuilders to produce vehicles such as hearses. At its peak, production reached around five cars per week and even at the very end all the cars made were pre-sold. The very last car was kept for the Jaguar-Daimler Heritage Trust collection.

The DS420 was killed off partly as a result of legislation (there was always difficulty in matching the regulations in many export markets) and partly because of production economies of scale. In short, it just became too expensive to build cars like the Daimler DS420, and in future the limousine market will be supplied with stretched versions of conventional saloons like the very latest Daimler Century.

Today DS420s have a loyal following as one of the last true coachbuilt cars. Their useability is all the greater now that several specialist firms have been set up around the country to cater for the maintenance, purchase and sale of the model.

As the years progressed, the DS420 (above) sacrificed many items of trim, such as its 'D' mascot, rimbellishers, overriders, rear quarterlights, and second chrome strip; front lighting was revised as well.

One of the very rare Landaulette bodies built by Vanden Plas, with its folding rear roof section. Many body/chassis units were supplied to outside coachbuilders for special bodies such as hearses.

If there is such a thing as a 'standard' rear compartment for the DS420, this is it. There may be no air conditioning or electric windows, but you still had leather, burr walnut and extra occasional seating.

SPECIFICATIONS

MAJESTIC MAJOR (1960-67)

Engine: 4561cc V8-cylinder overhead valve
Bore & stroke: 95 × 80mm
Power output: 220bhp at 5500rpm
Transmission: Borg Warner three-speed automatic
Wheelbase: 9ft 6in (289cm)
Length: 16ft 10in (513cm)/18ft 10in (574cm) limousine
Width: 6ft 1in (185cm)
Height: 5ft 2½in (159cm)/5ft 3½in (161cm) limousine
Weight: 37cwt (1880kg)/40cwt (2032kg) limousine
Suspension: Front: semi-trailing wishbones, coil springs, telescopic dampers. Rear: live axle, half elliptic springs, telescopic dampers
Brakes: Dunlop four-wheel discs, servo-assisted
Top speed: 120mph (192kmh)/110mph (176kmh) limousine
0-50mph (80kmh): 7 secs/9 secs limousine
Price new: £2995/£3800 limousine
Total Production: Saloon 1178; Limousine 863
Grand Total 2041

DS420 (1968-92)

Engine: 4235cc six-cylinder twin overhead camshaft
Bore & stroke: 92 × 106mm
Power output: 177bhp at 4750rpm
Transmission: Borg Warner three-speed automatic
Wheelbase: 11ft 9in (358cm)
Length: 18ft 5in (561cm)
Width: 6ft 4½in (194cm)
Height: 5ft 2½in (159cm)
Weight: 42cwt (2134kg)
Suspension: Front: independent, semi-trailing wishbones, coil springs, telescopic dampers. Rear: independent, lower wishbone/upper driveshaft link, radius arms, twin coil springs
Brakes: Four-wheel discs, servo-assisted
Top speed: 110mph (176kmh)
0-50mph (80kmh): 9 secs
Price new: £4425
Total Production: Limousines 4116; Special bodies 927
Grand Total 5043

CHAPTER THIRTEEN

MARK X/420G

1961-70

MARK X 3.8-LITRE (1962-64)

From Jaguar's birth, saloons had formed the basis of the company's profitability and prospects for expansion. The top-of-the-range saloons inspired the famous advertising line 'Grace, Space and Pace', and they continued to epitomise these words into the 1960s.

The Mark IX, the ultimate development of the original 1950 Mark VII, was getting rather staid by the beginning of the 1960s and Jaguar desperately needed to launch something entirely new to maintain its market position, particularly in the crucial North American market where biggest was best! Hot on the heels of the launch of the E-type in March 1961, Jaguar introduced its new flagship saloon at the London Motor Show in October of that year – the Mark X.

The Mark X was the largest Jaguar ever produced, weighing in at 37cwt and measuring 16ft 10in long and a massive 6ft 4in wide – the widest car ever produced in Britain up to that time. That accolade would later go to the XJ220 supercar. The massive bulk of the Mark X was disguised through clever detailing, and styling which was much lower and sleeker than the Mark IX.

Certain familiar Jaguar styling trademarks were retained (like the traditional style radiator grille, the chromium-plated window frames and the sloping boot), but generally the approach was thoroughly modern. The bonnet line was significantly lowered while the slimmer grille was deliberately sloped forward to give the impression of even less height. A modern four-headlamp treatment and twin traditional horn grilles helped to keep

the nose suitably imposing. The use of smaller 14in wheels helped to disguise the bulk of the car still further and fitted in well with trends in North America.

The bodyshell was fabricated using spot-welded steel pressings, its structural strength coming from two giant 7in box sections, the floor area also being stiffened by transverse boxes and other members extending forward to accommodate the engine/subframe and rearwards for the boot area. The whole structure was immensely strong and, over the years, the Mark X shell has stood the test of time better than most other Jaguar models.

Mechanically the Mark X used the familiar XK six-cylinder engine in straight-port head form almost exactly to XK150 3.8-litre 'S' specification, even down to the triple 2in SU carburettors, albeit with brand new manifolding. Producing 245bhp through either a conventional four-speed manual or Borg Warner DG automatic gearbox the Mark X was certainly no slouch.

Although retaining a developed form of the Mark 2 front suspension, the Mark X received the very latest independent rear end from the E-type (details of which appear in the next chapter). Four-wheel disc brakes were fitted with the unusual addition of mechanically operated Kelsey Hayes bellows assistance. Power-assisted steering was fortunately standard as it was essential in such a heavy car.

The Mark X displayed the usual high quality leather and walnut interior treatment with a new design of dashboard adapted from the Mark 2, but with an all-over veneer finish and curved end panels. The centre console incorporated the new vacuum operated heating/air controls; flanking it were the

Styling of the Mark X nears fruition, circa 1958. This wood-and-metal mock-up featured styling ideas which were eventually abandoned, although the size and profile are close to the production version.

two reclining split bench type front seats complete with separate central armrests.

In keeping with the previous models, the rear seat accommodation was cavernous with the added luxury of walnut picnic tables incorporating mirrors and separate heating controls for the rear footwells. The one point of criticism about the Mark X's interior was the use of very high sills both for structural strength and to allow the floorpan to drop lower to provide sufficient head room for its occupants. Unfortunately they also made getting in and out of the car rather awkward.

Despite the Mark X's excessive size and weight, the triple carb engine could propel the car to 120mph with a 0-60mph time of only 10.8 seconds for the automatic transmission version and less for the manual. The car remained in production virtually unchanged until 1964 when the model was upgraded with a larger engine.

The interior of the Mark X was probably the widest of any production car. Leather-and-walnut dash took its cues from the Mark 2. Note the high sill, which impeded entry.

MARK X 4.2-LITRE (1964-66)

In October 1964 the Mark X received the new 4235cc version of the XK engine at the same time as the E-type. Cylinders 1 and 6 were moved out slightly and 3 and 4 moved closer together to accommodate a 5.07mm increase in bore and there was a thicker webbed crankshaft, revised water jacketing, new pistons with revised rings, new inlet manifold, new cooling system and viscous coupling to the engine fan, which all added up to a major improvement in engine efficiency.

The main reason for the engine change came about because of a need to improve mid-range torque, and indeed the new unit delivered an extra 23lb ft over the 3.8-litre unit (although power output remained much as before). Performance was increased marginally, with a 0.5 second reduction in the 0-60mph time and a quoted 2mph increase in top speed. The extra torque shone through in the mid range, the 50-70mph time being cut from 9.3 seconds for the 3.8-litre to 7.6 seconds on the 4.2.

Along with an alternator as standard equipment, the new 4.2-litre engine also featured a revised Marles Varamatic type of power steering which allowed the steering ratio to alter as the wheel was turned. Braking also came in for improvement with the fitment of a conventional Dunlop servo making the system more efficient.

Another significant mechanical change was a brand

Succeeding the Mark X in 1966 was the 420G with subtle front end styling changes, new hub caps and the option of two-tone paint schemes, in which case no chrome side strip was fitted.

Dimensionally the Mark X was huge (above) but graceful flowing lines managed to hide its bulk to a certain extent. The 420G (below) had a prominent centre bar in its grille, indicators on the front wings and - since this is a single-colour car - a chrome strip along its waist to make it appear lower and disguise its bulk.

new four-speed all-synchromesh gearbox (with or without overdrive) or an upgraded Borg Warner Model 8 automatic 'box instead of the old DG.

Internally minor trim changes were carried out, the most significant of which was the fitment of a revised heating and ventilating system allowing the mixture of hot and cold air. Externally the only change was a new '4.2' badge on the boot lid.

At launch, the 4.2-litre Mark X offered excellent value for money, selling for around £150 less than the price in 1961. Despite this under half the total Mark X production were 4.2s.

A few limousine versions of the Mark X 4.2 litre were made to special order. Utilising the same bodyshell as the saloon, the limousine featured a manually operated centre division with a fixed front seat position and could also be supplied with a number of specialized fittings like a cocktail cabinet and so on.

420G (1966-70)

Concurrently with changes to other models in the Jaguar range, the Mark X was re-designated as the 420G in October 1966. The change in model name brought about no mechanical changes to the specification but there were changes in detail styling both inside and out.

The radiator grille received a prominent centre bar and side repeater indicator lenses were fitted to the leading edges of both front wings. A prominent chromium-plated waistline strip appeared on single-colour bodywork, the new model also becoming available with a limited choice of two-tone paintwork finishes with no chrome strip, simply a thin coachline separating the lower (lighter) colour from the upper (darker). New hub caps and revised badging on the boot completed the external changes.

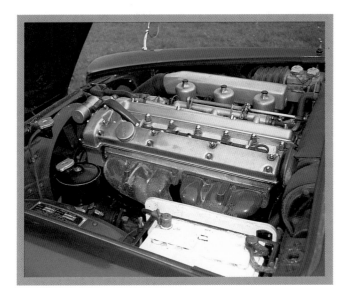

Triple-carb XK engine (above left) developed up to 265bhp in the Mark X and 420G but, with almost two tons to haul about, could not pretend to deliver sporting performance. An impressive sight: a sprawling array of instruments set in walnut (above right) and red leather from edge to edge made this a true luxury car. Padded top rail and centrally sited clock identify this as a 420G. The handful of Mark X/420G limousine versions (below) had a central glass division on top of fixed front seats and wall-to-wall veneer.

Inside, the 420G displayed the latest craze in aerated leather upholstery while a new padded top rail to the dashboard also included a centrally-mounted rectangular clock.

The 420G's price was kept competitive, launched at only £2238 in standard form. Although production soldiered on into mid-1970 (long after the introduction of the XJ6), a total of only 6500 420Gs were sold. As with the 4.2-litre Mark X, the 420G was also available with a limousine conversion but very few examples were ever produced.

The Mark X/420G range of models were never the most loved or respected of Jaguars, yet they offered a degree of luxury, performance and handling that bettered virtually anything else on the market at that time regardless of price. The arrival of their replacement, the XJ6, in 1968 would permanently overshadow the earlier cars.

SPECIFICATIONS

3.8-LITRE MARK X (1962-64)

Engine: 3781cc six-cylinder twin overhead camshaft
Bore & stroke: 87 × 106mm
Power output: 245bhp at 5500rpm
Transmission: Four-speed manual with or without overdrive, or Borg Warner three-speed automatic
Wheelbase: 10ft (305cm)
Length: 16ft 10in (513cm)
Width: 6ft 4in (193cm)
Height: 4ft 6½in (138cm)
Weight: 37cwt (1880kg)
Suspension: Front: independent, semi-trailing double wishbones, coil springs, anti-roll bar. Rear: independent, lower wishbones, upper driveshaft link, radius arms, twin coil springs
Brakes: Dunlop four-wheel discs, Kelsey Hayes vacuum servo
Top speed: 120mph (192kmh)
0-50mph (80kmh): 8.4 secs
Price new: £2392

MARK X 4.2-LITRE/420G (1964-70)

As 3.8-litre except:
Engine: 4235cc six-cylinder twin overhead camshaft
Bore & stroke: 92.07 × 106mm
Power output: 265bhp at 5400rpm
Brakes: Dunlop four-wheel discs, Dunlop servo assistance
Top speed: 122mph (195kmh)
0-50mph (80kmh): 7.9 secs
Price new: £2156
Total Production:
3.8-litre Mark X 12,678; 4.2-litre Mark X 5680; 420G 6554 **Grand Total** 25,212

CHAPTER FOURTEEN

E-TYPE 3.8-LITRE

1961-64

The original 1961 Geneva Show fixed head coupé with its exterior bonnet locks. The harmony and purposefulness of the E-type design was recognised from the outset.

After thirteen years of XK production, Jaguar badly needed to bring its sports car range up-to-date. This it did with a vengeance in the brand new E-type released to the public in March 1961 at the Geneva Motor Show.

The E-type represented a completely fresh sheet of paper. Although it bore a striking resemblance to the racing D-types of the 1950s, the new car embodied the very latest technology which put it at the forefront of sports car design in terms of refinement, handling and outright performance – indeed the E-type was virtually the fastest standard production car you could buy at the time.

Embodying wind-cheating aerodynamic styling, the E-type was unlike anything else in mass production at the time, utilising a monocoque type of construction of complex design. The hollow scuttle area met large hollow sills which projected forward towards the front wheels and continued rearward to meet a transverse hollow section ahead of the rear suspension. The floorpan provided further strength with a transverse

member running from side to side. Two more box sections ran underneath the floor from front to rear. At the rear the spare wheel well in the boot had two longitudinal box sections either side joining up with the rear cross member and the tail section, all of which held the rear suspension in situ.

At the front of the monocoque, a framework of square section steel tubing projected forwards to carry the front suspension and engine, which was bolted to the scuttle. Another smaller frame secured the radiator and bonnet supports.

The bonnet itself was a large single forward-hinged unit made up of smaller welded panels with a 'power bulge' down the centre to accommodate the top of the engine and louvered panels either side of the bulge to aid cooling. The front of the bonnet curved down to a large grilleless nose which incorporated faired-in headlamps.

From the outset the E-type was available in two versions. The first was a two-seater roadster with a proper foldaway hood, wind-up windows, a proper

E-type roadster (above) was more civilised than the XK150 roadster it replaced; the hood was permanently fixed to the car. Early roadster (below) with exterior bonnet locks and factory glassfibre hardtop.
White indicator lenses and whitewall tyres identify this as an export model.

boot area and the option of a factory-fitted hardtop made of glassfibre, effectively turning the car into a cosy grand touring coupé. Alternatively a two-seater fixed head coupé version was available with fastback rear styling incorporating a single side-hinged tailgate giving access to the boot area. The arrangement was rather like a mini-estate car.

Mechanically, the E-type owed little to the previous XK150 model in many ways but it did inherit the established XK six-cylinder engine in a single form, the triple SU carburettor 'S' version developing 265bhp at 5500rpm with a 9:1 compression ratio. Changes to specification included the fitment of an automatic choke system and a new style air filter mounted at

Early E-type production at Browns Lane took place
alongside Mark 2 saloons.

the side of the engine at sill level and ducted from the front of the bonnet. To keep the height of the unit to a minimum, a separate header tank was used between the radiator and engine and a thermostatically driven electric cooling fan replaced the normal engine-driven type.

Transmission was again carried over from the XK, using the four-speed Moss gearbox without overdrive (initially no automatic was available). On the suspension side, the front end used forged top and bottom wishbones, with an inner extension of the latter as an attachment for the torsion bar, which was anchored at its rear end to the bulkhead. Telescopic dampers and an anti-roll bar were also employed. The steering rack ran across

The E-type was virtually the fastest production sports car you could buy in 1961. To some controversy, British road testers managed to record a genuine 150mph in a roadster.

the car behind the radiator and the steering column was universal-jointed. Eleven inch front disc brakes were used, helped by the American-designed Kelsey Hayes mechanical system, as fitted to the Mark X saloon. Two master cylinders were fitted to the E-type.

For the rear end Jaguar developed something rather special, a system which would go on to be used in all other

As well as performing superlatively, the 3.8 also handles beautifully.

Jaguar sports and saloons cars with little change well into the 1990s: a complete assembly encapsulated in a

separate subframe. A Salisbury differential of a type similar to that used on other Jaguars was used, with Power-Lok limited slip, and was rigidly mounted in the steel subframe. Universally jointed half-shafts led to the hubs, which had light alloy casings. The casings were extended downward to pivots on which were attached the lower suspension links. These links were forked, attaching to the wheel hub casing at one end and to the subframe at the other.

The fixed head is every bit as beautiful as the roadster. Interestingly, the fixed head recorded a Cd figure of only 0.44, revealing it to be nowhere near as aerodynamic as its shape suggests.

Two coil spring/damper units were mounted on the lower suspension links and, at the top, to the sub-frame on either side of the differential unit. 10in inboard disc brakes were fitted directly on to the output shafts of the differential.

The whole rear subframe assembly was mounted to the bodywork via four angled bonded rubber mountings to prevent transference of noise, and by two trailing radius arms also fixed to the body via rubber mountings; there was also an anti-roll bar.

The huge bonnet swings forward in one piece.

The whole assembly provided no metal-to-metal contact with the body at all. All E-types came equipped as standard with 15in 72-spoke wire wheels with a rim width of five inches.

Although the E-type looked a much larger car than its predecessor, it was actually only 14ft 7½in long. It was much lower and wider than the XK but at the same time nearly 5cwt lighter. Performance was marginally improved over the XK150 3.8 'S' with a 0-50mph time of 5.6 seconds (over half a

The 3.8-litre 265bhp XK triple-carb engine fitted to the first E-types.

second faster) and a maximum speed of 150mph (as against about 140mph).

Internally the 3.8-litre E-type adopted a completely fresh approach, the dashboard layout taking some cues from the 1959 Mark 2 saloon. There was a total absence of wood, only moulded plastic with a crackle finish, plus vinyl and bright aluminium for the centre console and centre section of the

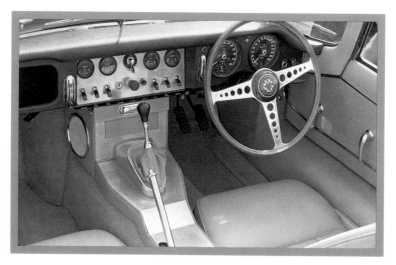

All 3.8 E-types feature evocative aluminium brightwork on the dashboard and centre console. There is no woodwork apart from the steering wheel rim, but plenty of leather.

instrument panel. Bucket seats, a fly-off handbrake and a very attractive three-spoke woodrim steering wheel all confirmed the E-type's sporting character. The view from the driver's seat along nearly seven feet of bulging bonnet was something to behold!

The E-type hit the road at a modest £2100 for the roadster and £2200 for the fixed head coupé, at a time when even the most mundane Ferrari (which could not outperform the E-type anyway) cost over twice that much.

The car took the world by storm, just as the original XK120 had done in 1948. So popular was this new Jaguar that initially cars were changing hands for premium prices. The E-type was well appreciated by competition drivers: Roy Salvadori, John Coombs, Graham Hill and many others raced the cars successfully during the early years of production.

The 3.8-litre E-type continued in full-scale production until 1964 when the model was upgraded mechanically in line with the Mark X.

Top down is the only way to travel in the roadster, conditions allowing; the hood is stowed under a protective cover.

The fixed head incorporates this extremely functional arrangement of an opening hatchback (left), allowing access to a surprisingly roomy luggage compartment.

SPECIFICATIONS

E-TYPE 3.8-LITRE (1962-64)

Engine: 3781cc six-cylinder twin overhead camshaft

Bore & stroke: 87mm × 106mm

Power output: 265bhp at 5500rpm

Transmission: Four-speed manual

Wheelbase: 8ft (244cm)

Length: 14ft 7½in (446cm)

Width: 5ft 4½in (164cm)

Height: 3ft 11in (119cm)

Weight: 24cwt (1219kg)

Suspension: Front: independent, wishbone, torsion bars, anti-roll bar. Rear: independent, lower wishbone, upper driveshaft link, radius arms, coil springs, anti-roll bar

Brakes: Dunlop four-wheel discs, Kelsey Hayes power assistance

Top speed: 150mph (240kmh)

0-50mph (80kmh): 5.6 secs

Price new: £2098

Total Production: Roadster 7827; Fixed Head 7669

Grand Total 15,496

CHAPTER FIFTEEN

E-TYPE 4.2-LITRE SERIES 1
1964-68

The 4.2-litre Series 1 E-type was indistinguishable externally from the 3.8 apart from badging on the boot lid but it had significantly improved gearchange, clutch, brakes and cooling.

From September 1964, the E-type 3.8-litre models were discontinued in favour of new models with the 4235cc engine also used in the Mark X and discussed in a previous chapter. Utilising the new block with revised bore centres, a new crankshaft, a modified water jacket to improve coolant flow, and new pistons with oil control rings, the bigger-capacity engine offered not only improved torque in the mid range (up 43lb ft to 283lb ft) but also improved oil consumption. Additionally, aluminised silencers were fitted to the exhaust for longer life. The engine also now had an alternator fitted as standard equipment and a pre-engaged starter.

To accompany the 4.2-litre engine, the 'new' E-type also took advantage of the revised Jaguar four-speed all-synchromesh gearbox with cast-iron casing and a new Laycock diaphragm spring clutch. The brakes were supplemented by a conventional vacuum servo and dust shields were fitted to the brake discs.

Externally the new E-type looked exactly the same as the 3.8 except for the '4.2' badging on the boot lid (roadster) or tailgate (fixed head). Internally the 4.2-litre E-types now had improved front seats with better support, and the bright aluminium on the centre console and dashboard had disappeared in favour of a more subdued black cloth finish. Additionally, the centre console now featured a fitted glove box and there was better trimming for the rear compartment of the fixed head coupé version.

Ultimate performance of the 4.2-litre E-types did not increase significantly, the 0-50mph time improving by only 0.8sec, with top speed unaffected at a fraction under 150mph. However, the car was much more torquey and pleasant to drive, helped by the all-synchromesh gearbox and better seating.

The price of the 4.2-litre E-type increased margin-

A new addition to the range in 1966 was the 2+2. Its wheelbase was 19in longer, the windscreen was less raked and the rear roof line was raised to increase interior space. The result was not quite so aesthetically pleasing.

The driving characteristics of the 4.2 altered: now there was more low-down torque and mid-range pull, while the gearbox changed from Moss to Jaguar manufacture.

Interior layout remained much as before but there was more leather, no aluminium, improved seating and an armrest between the front seats.

ally over the '64 model 3.8 and would continue in production with only minor changes until September 1968, when North American Federal regulations would force a further development of the E-type theme.

E - TYPE 2 + 2

The 4.2-litre range gained a third member during this production period, the brand new 2+2 which was launched in March 1966.

The reason behind this extra model was to entice a wider buying public to the E-type by offering a semi-four-seater based on the fixed head coupé bodyshell. Basically of exactly the same mechanical specification as the two-seater cars, the 2+2 gained an extra nine inches in the wheelbase, two inches in overall height and an extra 2cwt of weight at 27.7cwt.

The extra length in the body gave enough room for the fitment of two seats in the rear compartment for children or for the less frequent use of adult passengers, without sacrificing valuable luggage accommodation. The loftier glasshouse, created by increasing the height of the front screen by 1½in and inclining its rake more toward the vertical plane, was necessary to provide sufficient head room inside the car. Most of the extra length of the body was taken up by the floorpan, allowing the doors to be lengthened by 8½in for ease of access to the rear compartment.

Apart from the additional seats the only changes internally were the fitment of a full-width parcel tray under the dashboard, a larger glove box and an improved heating system.

To improve the ride and handling, both spring rates and dampers were uprated to allow for the likely extra payload and improved exhaust shielding was fitted to prevent heat entering the interior of the car. Mechanically the only other change was the avail-ability of Borg Warner automatic transmission for an additional £140.

£2245 would buy you a brand new 2+2 E-type in 1966, a mere £252 more than the equivalent two-seater. Out of 5598 2 + 2 Series 1 E-types produced, the majority were supplied in left-hand drive form and the car continued in production until the demise of the other Series 1s in favour of the Federally adapted Series 2 discussed below.

A grand total of 22,916 4.2-litre Series 1 E-types were made in a little over four years, 32 per cent more than the 3.8 – proving that, even after seven years in production, the E-type was still readily finding new customers who appreciated the timeless lines.

E - TYPE SERIES 1½ (1967-1968)

Jaguar produced an interim model in the E-type range, a mid-way development from the Series 1 4.2 to the Series 2 of 1968. Introduced progressively from 1967, the so-called Series 1½ was never strictly speaking marketed as anything different than a Series 1 but it incorporated significant changes in styling which anticipated the Series 2.

There is no such thing as a definitive Series 1½ specification as different cars display differing attributes of the earlier and later models. Most, however, featured open headlight units without cowled glass aerodynamic covers and consequently used different chromium surrounds. This move was forced on Jaguar by changing Federal regulations in North America. Despite this alteration, these cars retained the Series 1 style bonnet and bumper bar.

Internally, some Series 1½s continued to use Series 1 trim while others adopted the later Series 2 style switchgear. In all other respects these cars were the same as the Series 1 and were produced in all three body styles.

With its longer wheelbase, the 2+2 has plenty of room for an extra two seats for children. The seat back could be folded down to extend the luggage platform.

The 4.2 engine is externally identifiable by details like the ribbed air cleaner box. The cylinders were bored out and the result was a much wider spread of torque.

S P E C I F I C A T I O N S

E-TYPE 4.2-LITRE SERIES 1 (1964-1968)

As 3.8-litre except:
Engine: 4235cc six-cylinder twin overhead camshaft
Bore & stroke: 92.07mm × 106mm
Power output: 265bhp at 5400rpm
Transmission: Four-speed manual or Borg Warner three-speed automatic
Wheelbase: 8ft (244cm)/8ft 9in (267cm) 2+2
Length: 14ft 7in (444cm)/15ft 4½in (469cm) 2+2
Height: 4ft (122cm)/4ft 2½in (128cm) 2+2
Weight: 25cwt (1270kg)/27½cwt (1397kg) 2+2
Brakes: servo assistance
Top speed: 150mph (240kmh)/136mph (218kmh) 2+2
0-50mph (80kmh): 5 secs/6.8secs 2+2
Price new: £1992/£2245 2+2
Total Production:
4.2-litre Series 1 Roadster 9548
4.2-litre Series 1 Fixed Head 7770
4.2-litre Series 1 2+2 5598
Grand Total 22,916

The so-called Series '1½' was an interim model which incorporated some features of the Series 2, such as uncowled headlamps, with old-spec features including the bumpers and indicators. This interim model was produced only during 1967 and 1968.

E-TYPE SERIES 2
1968-70

The Series 2 E-type was launched in October 1968 at the Earls Court Motor Show. Externally many detail changes were made to satisfy North American Federal regulations which, at that time, were getting ever more complex and demanding for car manufacturers, particularly companies like Jaguar which were dependent on models designed several years previously.

A brand new bonnet was fitted, with a larger air intake nose section giving a 68 per cent increase in capacity to ensure sufficient cooling for the new emission-controlled XK engine. The new bonnet also incorporated headlamps repositioned 2in further forward and now completely open, ie. without the previous glass cowls. This arrangement minimised light scatter and also necessitated new plated surrounds (all of which differed from the earlier Series 1½ models). To accompany these changes new indicator side repeater lights were incorporated into the leading edge sides of the bonnet.

The use of chromium plating was extended, with full wrap-around bumpers and the fitment of larger, re-positioned front and rear side/flasher lights below bumper level, at the rear affixed to a full-width satin panel. Also at the rear, a new style square number plate mounting was used which in turn meant the exhaust pipes had to be repositioned further apart.

Although wire wheels were still available for the E-

Although many people thought its styling had been compromised by the fitment of Federal style lighting and bumpers, the Series 2 E-type was still a seminal sports car and sold better than ever.

The difference in profile between the two-seater (foreground) and 2+2 can be seen here. The 2+2's windscreen was further forward than the coupé's.

Chromed wire wheels were almost essential wear for the E-type, although the Series 2 could also now be had with steel disc wheels.

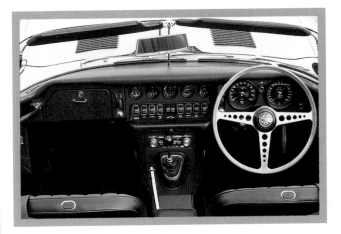

A separate centrally mounted clock and a row of rocker switches updated the Series 2 dash, and there was now a lid for the glove box.

type, these were now of the new 'easy clean' type with flat centre hubs, in either chromium plate or stove-enamelling. As a further option, for the first time an E-type became available with chromium-plated steel wheels with conventional hub caps, which proved popular.

Mechanically, the 4.2-litre XK engine was modified to cope with ever-stricter Federal emission regulations for imported cars. To improve the cooling capability,

two electrically-driven thermostatically-controlled fans were employed. Although the Series 2 E-types retained triple SU carburettors for the home market, North American cars had twin Stromberg C 'emission' carburettors with cross-over inlet manifold, drastically reducing the car's overall performance. The brakes were uprated with a larger pad area and three brake pistons at the front and two at the rear. North American tastes were also responsible for the Series 2 going

As well as the roadster and 2+2 body styles, the Series 2 continued with the two-seater fixed head shape, seen here in US trim with side repeater lights, amber parking lights and whitewall tyres.

The Series 2 incorporated a larger 'mouth' in the bonnet, exposed headlights and side and indicator lights mounted under the bumper.

The Series 2 had a centre section to the higher bumper, reshaped exhaust pipes and an anodised panel for the rear lights and number plate plinth.

'soft' on the equipment front, with not only automatic transmission continuing as an option for the 2+2 but, for the first time ever, air conditioning and even power steering options! As an early attempt to improve interior safety the Series 2 sprouted rocker switches for all the ancillary controls, replacing the usual toggles, while the door handles were redesigned and recessed into the trim panels. An integrated ignition/starter switch on the key eliminated the black push-button so well known on all previous Jaguars.

The Series 2 cars were introduced at a modestly increased price over the Series 1: £2163 for the roadster, £2273 for the fixed head coupe and £2512 for the

2 + 2 in standard trim. Just under 19,000 were made in total over a production run of only 23 months. According to factory records, production of the Series 2 cars finished in September 1970 which meant there was a break in production of E-types between this time and the launch of the revised Series 3 in 1971.

Although to many purists the Series 2 E-type was never as aesthetically pleasing as the earlier cars, production levels and sales increased in the late 1960s, proving that it was highly regarded at the time. The E-type could certainly not have continued on sale in North America if the Series 2 changes had not kept the car ahead of legislation.

The 4.2-litre engine of the S2 had twin electric cooling fans. This is an American specification engine with twin Stromberg carbs in place of triple SUs. The US emissions control equipment drastically reduced power output.

Where air conditioning was specified for North America, ducting was added to the lower dash panel.

S P E C I F I C A T I O N S

E-TYPE 4.2-LITRE SERIES 2 (1968-70)

Engine: 4235cc six-cylinder twin overhead camshaft
Bore & stroke: 92.07mm × 106mm
Power output: 265bhp at 5400rpm
Transmission: Four-speed manual (or Borg Warner three-speed automatic for 2+2)
Wheelbase: 8ft (244cm)/8ft 9in (267cm) 2+2
Length: 14ft 7in (444cm)/15ft 4½in (469cm) 2+2
Width: 5ft 6in (168cm)
Height: 4ft (122cm) Fixed Head/4ft 2½in (128cm) 2+2
Weight: 25cwt (1270kg)/27½cwt (1397kg) 2+2
Suspension: Front: independent, wishbones, torsion bar, anti-roll bar. Rear: independent, lower wishbone, upper driveshaft link, radius arms, coil springs, anti-roll bar
Brakes: Dunlop four-wheel discs, servo assistance
Top speed: 150mph (240kmh)/136mph (218kmh) 2+2
0-50mph (80kmh): 5 secs/6.8secs 2+2
Price new: £2163/£2512 2+2
Total Production:
4.2-litre Series 2 Roadster 8627
4.2-litre Series 2 Fixed Head 4855
4.2-litre Series 2 2+2 5326
Grand Total 18,808

CHAPTER SEVENTEEN

E-TYPE SERIES 3
1971-75

The final development of the E-type was announced on 29th March 1971, amazingly over five months after the end of production of the Series 2. The reason for this was to allow time to clear stocks of Series 2s, whose sales had been dwindling, while the Series 3 took longer to develop than expected. When the Series 3 finally did arrive, it put the E-type back on top in the sports car field.

Jaguar had already built a quad overhead camshaft 5-litre 500bhp 12-cylinder engine which was fitted to the XJ13 sports-racing prototype, and this could well have been considered for the next generation E-type, but its complexity would have led to major production difficulties.

Instead Jaguar invested over £3 million in developing a new V12 engine and machine shop facilities, not only for the E-type but also for Jaguar's new saloon model, the XJ6. The new engine's first use was in the revised and uprated version of the E-type, the Series 3, effectively as a test-bed, just as the XK120 had been back in 1948 for the six-cylinder engine.

The new V12 featured a single overhead camshaft for each bank of six cylinders, operating in-line valves within a flat cylinder head, the compression chambers being housed in the recessed piston crowns. Of 5343cc capacity with a bore and stroke of 90mm and 70mm, the production engine had a cast alu-

minium block and heads which meant an increase of only 80lb in weight over the old XK six-cylinder unit. The V12 engine featured no less than four Stromberg CD carburettors set in pairs outside the 60 degree 'V' formation.

The V12 used the then-new Lucas OPUS electronic ignition system with electro-magnetic pick-up and solid state electronics. Despite such high technology Jaguar continued to use chain drive to the two camshafts.

The maximum torque from the new engine was 304lb ft at 3600rpm and it developed 272bhp at 5850rpm, providing a significant boost in performance over the old car. The 0-60mph time improved on the manual transmission car from 7.1 seconds for the original 3.8-litre down to 6.4 seconds for the V12. Nearly two seconds were taken off the 0-100mph time when compared to the 4.2-litre engined car, although top speed remained virtually the same at just under the 150mph mark.

To cope with the extra weight (28.8cwt for the roadster) and the improved performance the V12, the Series 3 sat on massive E70 VR15 tyres on 6in rims, either chromium-plated steel or conventional wire wheels in stove enamel or chrome finishes.

The Series 3 E-type was available either with the Borg Warner Model 12

Series 3 E-type's modified front end, wheelarches and fatter wheels and tyres made it distinctive. The 2+2 was your only choice if you wanted an S3 with a fixed roof.

Series 3 on location at Warwick Castle. The roadster was very different from any previous incarnation because it came on the longer wheelbase only. The chrome-plated disc wheels were a carry-over from the S2.

three-speed automatic transmission (now for the first time on the roadster as well as the fixed head) or with a Jaguar four-speed all-synchromesh gearbox and a larger diameter clutch.

The front subframe of the E-type had to be redesigned to accommodate the mass and torque of the V12 engine which also involved strengthening the bulkhead and the addition of a front tie bar. The front suspension was also uprated to incorporate the anti-dive geometry of the new XJ6 (discussed in a later chapter). Braking was improved by fitting ventilated discs at the front and the provision of air scoops under the bodywork to direct air to the inboard rear discs and assist cooling.

The Series 3 E-type was built on the extended floor-pan of the 2+2 models for both the roadster and the fixed head coupé, the latter always being a 2+2 con-figuration, which effectively reduced the range of models by one (the two-seater fixed head). With a completely redesigned bonnet with broader front wings and wheelarches to accommodate the fatter tyres and wider wheels, there was also an enlarged nose intake with chromium-plated grille and under-scoop to aid cooling of the massive V12 engine. Head-lights were again of the open type but of slightly dif-ferent design to the Series 2.

Moving rearwards, the roadster and coupé now

Jaguar's new V12 – the first volume-produced V12 since 1948 – was first seen in the E-type. It was smooth, flexible and refined, but a squeeze under the bonnet.

With the V12 engine as a standard fitment, the E-type was now in a different class in terms of acceleration and flexibility. Its wider set wheels and larger tyres gave much improved grip.

The Series 3 interior remained very similar to the Series 2's, although the switches and some gauges were new. This is a manual car, but automatic was also available.

All Series 3 E-types had this revised nose treatment: wide 'egg-crate' grille, improved lighting and a prominent air scoop below the grille.

used the 2+2 door frames and the rear wheelarches were also modified to accommodate the fatter tyres. Rear end styling was also altered, the most notable feature being the four exhaust pipes of an unusual flattened appearance. Both the boot of the roadster and the tailgate of the coupé employed prominent new 'V12' chromium-plated badging.

The Series 3 cars were 8½in longer and both wider and heavier than their predecessors but nevertheless were still well proportioned and retained the distinctive E-type themes that had captivated such a wide audience back in 1961.

Internally the Series 3 only came in for minor improvements. The brand new, smaller diameter aluminium spoked steering wheel now had a leather rather than wood rim, the heating and demisting system was improved, and on the fixed head an extractor duct was fitted in the tailgate. Slight changes in seating

The very last E-type made, finished in black paintwork with a commemorative plaque on the dashboard signed by Sir William Lyons.
Note the factory glassfibre hardtop.

were carried out and there were revised door trims and instruments.

Prices at launch were £3123 for the roadster and £3369 for the 2+2 fixed head. Initially a six-cylinder XK-engined Series 3 E-type was also listed but it is understood that only a couple were ever actually supplied. In total over 15,000 Series 3 E-types were produced, over 80 per cent of which went to the North American market. After an upsurge in E-type sales in 1974, this tailed off dramatically leading to the announcement that production of the E-type would cease in February 1975.

The very last 50 cars, all right-hand drive, were signed off with the addition of a special brass commemorative plaque affixed to the dashboard signed by Sir William Lyons himself, 49 of the cars being finished specially in black paintwork.

The demise of the E-type effectively ended Jaguar's production of true sports cars. Since that time the Series 3 has perhaps become the most sought-after of all E-types, particularly in roadster form. Indeed it was a V12 roadster which broke the £100,000 price barrier for a classic E-type in the heady classic car boom of the late 1980s.

S P E C I F I C A T I O N S

E-TYPE SERIES 3 V12 (1971-75)

Engine: 5343cc V12-cylinder, single overhead camshaft per bank
Bore & stroke: 90 × 70mm
Power output: 272bhp at 5850rpm
Transmission: Four-speed all-synchromesh manual or Borg Warner three-speed automatic
Wheelbase: 8ft 9in (267cm)
Length: 15ft 4in (467cm)
Width: 5ft 6½in (168cm)
Height: 4ft 1in (124cm)
Weight: 29cwt (1473kg)
Suspension: Front: independent, wishbones, torsion bars, anti-roll bar. Rear: independent, lower wishbones, upper driveshaft link, radius arms, coil springs and anti-roll bar
Brakes: Girling four-wheel discs, ventilated at front, servo assistance
Top speed: 146mph (234kmh)
0-50mph (80kmh): 4.7 secs
Price new: £3123/£3369
Total Production: V12 Series 3 Roadster 7990; V12 Series 3 Fixed Head 7297
Grand Total 15,287

CHAPTER EIGHTEEN

S-TYPE & 420

1963-69

During Jaguar's expansionary period of the 1960s it was seeking other market niches and there seemed an obvious gap between the flagship Mark X saloon and the compact sporting Mark 2 saloon. Working as before on the premise of cutting overheads and bringing down unit costs of production it seemed natural to develop a further intermediate model or models to fill the void – enter the S-type.

S-TYPE (1963-68)

Maintaining elements of the general style of both the Mark 2 and Mark X saloons, the S-type used the basic floorpan and centre structure of the Mark 2 although significant strengthening was needed to accommodate independent rear suspension. The centre section of the bodywork was copied almost directly from the Mark 2 although the roof section was flatter, the rear window much larger and the door frames and locks slightly different.

At the front, from a distance you could almost be looking at a Mark 2 but in fact everything was different save for the bonnet pressing, bonnet centre chrome strip and leaping cat mascot. Subtly different shaping to the front wings incorporated eyelids to the headlights, wrap-around indicator lenses, re-positioned side lights and new-style recessed fog/spot lights. Gone were the heavily-ribbed bumpers found on the Mark 2 in favour of a slim-line style with neater over-riders. Finally the radiator grille was given a more prominent chrome surround and centre vane.

At the rear, the S-type derived its styling (though not its panelling) from the Mark X, giving a new corporate identity to Jaguar rear end styling in the mid-1960s. A longer, flatter boot panel with flowing wings incorporated all-new lighting and again the slim-line bumper treatment. The twin-pipe exhaust system now exited separately and centrally (*à la* Mark X), as opposed to being closely set and part of the same one-piece system as on the Mark 2.

Internally the traditional wood and leather treatment continued, but again with subtle changes, taking

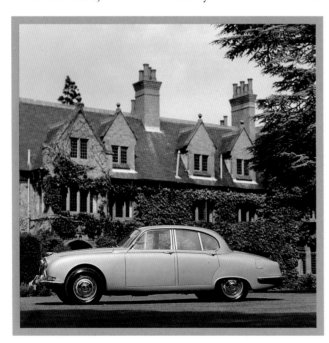

The S-type was an early example of niche marketing, filling a small gap between the Mark 2 and Mark X. This is a 3.4-litre model with standard steel wheels.

The style of the S-type's interior was an amalgam of Mark 2 and Mark X. Seating was unique to the S-type and was inspired by the Daimler 2.5-litre V8 saloon.

Four headlamps, a squared-off nose and upright grille for the 420, introduced in 1966, set it apart from the Mark 2 style S-type frontal treatment.

a lead from the Mark X. Although retaining the corporate dashboard layout, the centre (auxiliary switch/instrument) panel was now finished in veneer like the larger car and the facia incorporated more curves. With minor switch and trim changes, the centre console also now took on a more curved style and the front seats were brand new, inspired by yet another model variant – the Daimler V8 saloon. Although still separate, the front seats were effectively a split bench-style with individual centre arm-rests; new adjustment mechanisms were employed and the seats were now much thinner because there were no rear picnic tables.

Rear seating was similarly styled and again thinner which meant slightly more room for rear seat passengers (although overall dimensions internally were hardly any different from a Mark 2). Door trim panels were also restyled and the headlining was of the stretched nylon type, again like the Mark X.

As far as the engine, transmission and front axle lay-out were concerned, everything came directly from the Mark 2 but, because the S-type was aimed slightly more up-market, it was only ever offered with the 3.4- or 3.8-litre engines. Brakes were slightly uprated, with revised Dunlop calipers but the big change came at the rear. The S-type featured the independent rear suspension layout of the E-type and Mark X, with inboard disc brakes and enclosed cage assembly, although with certain amendments to make it fit the smaller bodyshell.

Launched in October 1963 at £1669, the S-type was promoted as a car for the businessman who wanted the turn of speed, comfort, controlled ride and style of a Jaguar without the overtly sporting image of the Mark 2 or the extravagance of the Mark X. The S-type offered slightly more comfort, a much better ride quality and more boot space than the former, and better economy and agility, with less bulk, than the latter.

It was a relatively successful model for Jaguar, with total production amounting to over 25,000 examples by August 1968. Latterly the S-type received the same set of 'economy' measures as the Mark 2, standard specification cars having Ambla instead of leather upholstery.

420 (1966-68)

By 1966 Jaguar was in full expansion. Even with the intermediate S-type offering more opportunities to sell cars, Jaguar saw the need for a further saloon and so developed the 420 model, which was released in October 1966.

Aimed squarely at existing Jaguar customers thinking of upgrading to a better model without going to the extremes of the Mark X, the 420 entered the fray at around £1930, nearly £200 dearer than the 3.8 S-type. The 420 was self-evidently a descendant of the S-type, its middle and rear bodywork being exactly the same (save for the badging). The front, however, owed more to the Mark X, with flatter front wings and bonnet, four headlights and a squatter radiator grille.

From the rear, the S-type looks like a Mark 2 centre hull grafted on to a Mark X rear end, which is not far off how the car was developed.

The interior was also predominantly S-type with subtle changes here and there, such as the fitment of a modicum of crash padding in the form of black Ambla to the dashboard top rail, which also incorporated a 420G-style square clock. Thinner wood cappings were used for the doors, another trend which would eventually follow on other Jaguar saloons.

Mechanically the 420 (as the model name intimated) used the 4235cc XK six-cylinder power unit although in a detuned form with only two SU carburet-

The 420's dashboard differed from the S-type's in having a black padded Ambla dash top rail and Mark X style square clock. This automatic model has a column shift.

tors instead of the three found in the E-type and Mark X. This change also necessitated the design of new inlet manifolding, while an improved cooling system was incorporated. This variant of the XK engine was rated at 245bhp.

Transmission was via the conventional Jaguar four-speed manual gearbox (with or without overdrive) or the Borg Warner Model 8 three-speed automatic with D1 and D2 drive positions. Conventional Burman recirculating ball steering continued, with the option of Marles Varamatic power assistance taken from the Mark X. Girling disc brakes all round incorporated twin circuits, again taken from the big Jaguar.

DAIMLER SOVEREIGN (1966-69)

Interestingly, Jaguar's 420 was the first to become available as a badge-engineered Daimler equivalent. At least with the Daimler 2.5-Litre V8, the Mark 2 lookalike had its own engine; now even the Jaguar engine would be incorporated albeit with a Daimler badge on the cam covers! Released at the same time as the Jaguar 420, the Daimler variant was called the Sovereign, a model name which would go on to become synonymous with Daimler models until 1984. The Daimler offered exactly the same standard of trim as the 420, although discreet 'D' badging featured on areas like the horn boss of the steering wheel. Power steering was standard rather than an extra-cost option and, if manual transmission was specified, it always came with overdrive as standard on Daimler models.

Externally the Sovereign featured a traditional Daimler fluted radiator grille, fluted rear number plate nacelle, Daimler badging and 'D' insignia on the hub caps. The Daimler Sovereign commanded a rather more lofty price than the Jaguar 420 at £2198, a mere £40 less than Jaguar's top-of-the-range Mark X at the time!

As far as performance was concerned, the 420 and Sovereign offered an improvement over the 3.8-litre S-type: the 0-60mph time was cut by 0.3 seconds and,

The fluted grille, bonnet mascot, badges and hubcap insignia are the only signs that this is a Daimler Sovereign, a badge-engineered version of the Jaguar 420. It actually outlasted the Jaguar 420, which had been displaced in 1968 by the arrival of the new XJ6.

more significantly, the 0-100mph time came down to 27.4 seconds, wiping nearly 4.5 seconds off the S-type's time. Fuel economy was practically the same, however.

The 420 and Sovereign had a relatively small production run of only 15,630 examples. Interestingly, the Jaguar version suffered an early demise due to the announcement of the new Jaguar XJ6 in September 1968 yet the Sovereign model continued on into 1969 until the Daimlerised version of the XJ6 became available, again badged as the Sovereign.

Perhaps the 420 was nothing more than a stop-gap model while the all-new XJ6 was still undergoing development. Certainly the 420 has always tended to be overshadowed by Jaguar's more charismatic Mark 2. It is very much under-rated when one considers that it offered everything that the Mark 2 and 'S' Type did plus added performance and more up-to-date styling.

S P E C I F I C A T I O N S

S-TYPE 3.4/3.8-LITRE (1963-1968)

Engine: 3442cc/3781cc six-cylinder twin overhead camshaft
Bore & stroke: 83 × 106mm/87 × 106mm
Power Output: 210bhp at 5500rpm/220bhp at 5500rpm
Transmission: Four-speed manual with or without overdrive, or Borg Warner three-speed automatic
Wheelbase: 8ft 11½in (273cm)
Length: 15ft 7in (475cm)
Width: 5ft 6½in (168cm)
Height: 4ft 7¾in (142cm)
Weight: 32/33cwt (1626/1676kg)
Suspension: Front: independent, semi-trailing double wishbones, coil springs, anti-roll bar. Rear: independent, lower wishbones, upper driveshaft link, radius arms, twin coil springs
Brakes: Dunlop four-wheel discs, vacuum assisted
Top speed: 120mph (192kmh)
0-50mph (80kmh): 9.6 secs/7.5 secs
Price New: £1669/£1758
Total Production: S-type 3.4-litre 10,036; S-type 3.8-litre 15,135; **Grand Total** 25,171

420/SOVEREIGN (1966-1969)

Engine: 4235cc six-cylinder twin overhead camshaft
Bore & stroke: 92.07 × 106mm
Power output: 245bhp at 5500rpm
Transmission: Four-speed manual with or without overdrive, or Borg Warner three-speed automatic
Wheelbase: 8ft 11¾in (274cm)
Length: 15ft 7½in (476cm)
Width: 5ft 7in (170cm)
Height: 4ft 8¼in (143cm)
Weight: 33cwt (1676kg)
Suspension: Front: independent, semi-trailing double wishbones, coil springs, anti-roll bar. Rear: independent, lower wishbones, upper driveshaft link, radius arms, twin coil springs
Brakes: Dunlop four-wheel discs, vacuum assisted
Top speed: 123mph (197kmh)
0-50mph (80kmh): 7 secs
Price New: £1930
Total Production: 420 9801; Sovereign 5829;
Grand Total 15,630

CHAPTER NINETEEN

XJ SERIES 1
1968-73

Perhaps William Lyons' most complete car was the brilliant XJ6. For a luxury car, it was decidedly sporting and modern yet traditional. Small wonder it became 'Car of the Year'.

The year 1968 was to see the realisation of a new Jaguar policy: a single saloon car in the form of the XJ6. The company's first completely new saloon since the introduction of the Mark X in 1961, the XJ6 cost some £6 million in development. Launched at the October 1968 Earls Court Motor Show, the XJ6 put Jaguar firmly back at the forefront of saloon car design; a fact recognised by its winning of several accolades in the motoring world, not least of which was the Car of the Year Award.

The XJ6 despatched into the history books the 340, S-type and 420, although the 240, Daimler 250, 420G and Daimler Sovereign soldiered on in ever decreasing numbers until late 1969.

The biggest revolution for Jaguar was the bodyshell which was new in every respect, although it maintained the nebulous quality of the Jaguar 'look'. Perhaps one of the most controversial aspects was the radiator grille. Gone were the vertical bars and heavy chrome surround associated with Jaguar to be replaced by a birdcage style criss-cross of slats. The whole effect was quite striking but even more controversial was the removal of the leaping cat mascot from the bonnet, upsetting the purists and traditionalists. This 'cat-stration' was apparently done to satisfy increasingly stringent regulations abroad over the use of such adornments. Four headlights were supplemented by new-style side and indicator lighting, new

The greatest advance of the XJ series was in its chassis engineering, which endowed it with hitherto unknown handling prowess for a saloon. Refinement and performance were also excellent, at least in the 4.2-litre version.

horn grilles and slim-line bumpers.

Forward-mounted hinges for the one-piece bonnet were carried over from the Mark X/420G but here again the panelling was all-new. A centre bulge in the bonnet was forced by the much lower line of the styling and the height of the 4.2-litre XK engine. Less bulbous front wings with large wheelarch lips featured leaping cat mascots on their lower quarters.

Some prototypes were built with 420G roof sections but in the event a fresh approach was taken. The glass areas were all larger but the typical Jaguar chromium-plated window frames were retained. A relatively squared-off rear end managed to continue a Jaguar family 'look' again. A very flat boot panel and kicked-up leading edges of the rear wings made the shape distinctive. There was all-new lighting with reflectors and reversing lights either side of the boot lid and the number plate lights were

All XJs had an impressively luxurious interior. Although leather was now an option on most models, there was still wood veneer and plenty of standard equipment. Automatics were more popular than manuals.

positioned on the bumper bar. Another change for Jaguar was the use of a rectangular rear numberplate, not seen on any other post-1950 saloon up to that time. Finally a very simple chromium 'winged' decal surrounded the boot lock, along with new badging either side of the number plate on the vertical plane of the boot lid panel. The exhaust pipes emerged through holes in the pronounced bolt-on under-valance.

Through judicious use of strengthening techniques, the XJ6 bodyshell was stronger than the Mark X's. It is also worth mentioning that the very first examples of the XJ6 never carried a 'Jaguar' script anywhere on the car!

The proportions of the XJ6 were certainly better balanced than the Mark X and dimensions had been reduced in almost every area. The length decreased by nearly a foot, width by nearly seven inches, height by 1½in, and weight by 4cwt.

Inside the cabin the XJ6 also benefited from myriad improvements. The dashboard was typical 1960s with the two major instruments in front of the driver and ancillary gauges and switches placed on a separate central panel. The instruments, however, had chromium-plated bezels and rocker switches replaced the old toggle variety. Plenty of wood veneer remained but use was made of a plastic ribbed background to the minor instruments and there were thinner cappings to the tops of the doors.

The centre console was retained but used bright aluminium pressings as finishers, a throw-back to the original E-types of 1961. As well as parcel shelving under the dashboard, an oddments tray was provided in the centre

Rear view of 4.2-litre XJ6 emphasises its low waist line and the pronounced 'kick' in the top of the rear wing. This early example has straight exhaust tailpipes; later ones switched to curved tailpipes to prevent the backdraught of fumes.

console which terminated in a large central armrest which opened up to reveal a further storage area. Naturally there was still a traditional glove box on the passenger side of the dashboard. All-new seats with better cushioning featured ventilated leather facings (as on the 420G), and flush-fitting door handles and new door panelling trims also updated the interior layout, but you no longer got picnic tables.

Face-level ventilation was provided on both sides of the dashboard and separately for the rear seat passengers, part of a new sophisticated heating and ventilation system specifically designed for the XJ6 in the form of a Delaney Galley heating and ventilation unit which gave increased heat output to 5.5kW and increased airflow. Temperature could be 'dialed up' by the driver on a separate control which automatically maintained the temperature by thermostatic means. The driver could also alter the volume of heat by a separate control. All operations were carried out by a series of vacuum systems. Air extraction was also novel, featuring a one-way extractor vent in the rear parcel shelf. Air conditioning was now more readily available on the XJ6 than it had been on previous Jaguar saloons.

Mechanically speaking, the XJ6 looked, on paper at least, like an amalgam of previous models. The rear

suspension was taken directly from the Mark X and E-type with inboard disc brakes and separate subframe assembly. At the front end the basic engineering of previous Jaguars was retained, although now mounted on a substantial cross-member via rubber mounts which doubled up as mountings for the engine. The overall effect was to damp road noise down to the absolute minimum. Further, by inclining the upper wishbone pivot upwards and the lower downwards, the suspension optimised 'anti-dive' attributes under hard braking. Another change was the fitment of shock absorbers outside the springs.

The new steering system for the XJ6 was rack-and-pinion (the first ever on a Jaguar saloon) and was developed by the AdWest company to incorporate the Varamatic power steering system. The steering mechanism was mounted behind the suspension, enhancing safety in case of frontal impact.

Brakes at the rear were as on other Jaguars but for the front an improved three-piston system was used for the calipers. This decreased the likelihood of fade and improved pad life. A twin-circuit system was retained along with servo operation and a tandem master cylinder.

In association with Jaguar, Dunlop developed completely new tyres for the XJ6 in the form of SP Sport E70 VR15 radials, which provided a wider tread area, and although this increased road noise levels the XJ6 still boasted the best standards of noise suppression of any car in the world due to the joint efforts of the tyre manufacturers and chassis engineers.

Although it was designed from the outset to take the forthcoming V12 power unit, the XJ6 was launched with a choice of two configurations of the good old XK six cylinder unit. The 4.2-litre (by far the more popular) was taken virtually unmodified from the existing 420 saloon, utilising twin SU HD 8 carburettors (or Strombergs for the North American market). Engine cooling, however, had been dramatically improved by an enlarged impeller for the water pump, a bigger bypass hose and larger transfer holes in the cylinder head gasket on the exhaust valve side to maintain even temperatures. A 12-blade fan plus cross-flow radiator with separate header tank completed the changes in this area. Maximum power was the same as on the 420, around 245bhp.

The other engine for the XJ6 was of 2.8 litres capacity, strategically putting the size just below some European countries' tax break points. The make-up of the cylinder head was exactly as the 4.2-litre engine even down to the twin 2in SU carburettors. With a bore and stroke of 83mm × 86mm, it was rated at 180bhp at 6000rpm with 182lb ft of torque. As such it was somewhat underpowered in a car of the XJ's bulk.

Both engines were driven through the same Jaguar four-speed all-synchromesh gearbox with or without overdrive (the overdrive switch was placed on top of the gear knob), although the ratios were obviously different according to engine size. Alternatively, automatic transmission could be requested on either model, Borg Warner Type 35 for the 2.8-litre, Borg Warner Model 8 for the 4.2-litre.

Along with the normally highly-specified 2.8 and 4.2 XJ6s, Jaguar also initially offered a 'Standard' model with the 2.8-litre engine only. This was more than a little austere, with Ambla instead of leather upholstery, no rear seat arm-rest, a revised centre console without rear heater duct, no door pockets, no power steering and other minor trim omissions. The standard model cost £1797 but it is not known exactly how many (if any) were actually produced. In any case the better-equipped 2.8 cost only £1897, but it was the 4.2-litre at £2314 which proved most popular, showing that Jaguar's reputation for value for money had not been sacrificed.

The XK engine (above) persisted in the XJ6, seen here in 4.2-litre form (there was also a 2.8) with twin carburettors and a manual-with-overdrive gearbox. For the North American market, the 4.2 engine (below) was fitted with emissions-controlled twin Stromberg carbs and an exhaust-heated air system.

DAIMLER SOVEREIGN

Although the XJ was initially launched only as a Jaguar it wasn't long before the badge engineers got to work to produce a Daimler version named the Sovereign. This replaced the existing 420-based Sovereign and was introduced towards the end of 1969.

Fundamentally a Jaguar in every way, the Sovereign did, of course, feature the traditionally fluted radiator grille, which looked far more at home on the XJ6's front than Jaguar's 'egg crate' design. The fluting continued at the rear, on the boot-mounted casting surrounding the boot lock. External badging was also amended, even down to the hub cap insignia.

Internally, minor changes took place to the trim in an effort to differentiate the models, and purchasers of manual transmission models benefited from standard overdrive, although most cars produced were in fact automatics. The introduction of the new Daimler XJ-based

The Daimler version was simply a badge-engineered XJ, but its fluted grille looked better than the 'egg-crate' style of the Jaguar. Sixteen thousand of the 98,000 XJ Series 1 cars produced were Daimlers, from Sovereign 2.8-litre to Double-Six Vanden Plas.

Sovereign marked the end of production of all the old Jaguar saloons models like the 420G, leaving the XJ to meet the demands of all buyers.

XJ12/DOUBLE SIX

In July 1972 one of the most important developments of the XJ saloon took place with the launch of the 12-cylinder version, the XJ12. The all-aluminium V12 (described in more detail in the E-type Series 3 chapter) produced no less than 253bhp at 6000rpm. Even in the large saloon body, this meant staggering performance figures: for example, a 0-50mph time of 5.9 seconds (compared with 7.6 seconds for an automatic XJ6 4.2) and a maximum speed of well above 140mph. The penalty was very heavy fuel consumption: typically the mpg figure could drop into single figures!

Originally seen in the Series 3 E-type from 1971, the V12 was only slightly modified to fit the XJ body.

In 1972 came the launch of the 5.3-litre XJ12. The only external differences were the tasteful vertical slatted grille (with a 'V' motif), badging and wider tyres.

Because of the extra weight of the V12 engine, new higher rate springs were used on the car. The ventilated disc brake system from the E-type was also employed, complete with a balance valve to stop the rear wheels locking up, and an additional vacuum servo was accommodated in the front right-hand wing.

The massive V12 power unit with its four Stromberg carburettors, electronic ignition, usually an air conditioning compressor and many other ancillaries, certainly filled the engine bay of the XJ, which inevitably caused heat dissipation problems for Jaguar. This was addressed in several ways. Firstly, the battery tended to overheat so was fitted with its own thermostatically controlled electric cooling fan! Secondly, a massive cross-flow radiator with two distinct sections (and oil cooler) was employed to cool the four gallons of circulating coolant. Thirdly, to supplement the 17in Torquatrol engine-driven fan, a further

V12-powered XJs could lay a strong claim to being the best cars in the world in 1972. This is the ultimate Daimler Double Six Vanden Plas, opulent in the extreme and boasting a superb finish. Identification features were the Everflex vinyl roof, chrome strips, fog lamps and special badging.

smaller electro-thermostatically driven fan was employed. Jaguar also cleverly designed stainless steel shields to protect such items as the engine mountings, steering rack and floorpan of the car, while the exhaust downpipes were also double skinned.

Dunlop developed a new version of its XJ6 Sport tyre with a steel breaker strip to help carry the V12's extra weight, and Jaguar fitted new-style ventilated disc wheels to aid cooling of the brakes. In many cases these were chromium-plated.

As far as the transmission was concerned, V12 saloons were only ever

Inside, the Vanden Plas had leather, extra walnut, better carpets and separate rear seats, justifying its much higher price of £5368.

XJ6's bright aluminium). All XJ12s had a manual choke system, a beautifully engineered choke pull handle was accommodated below the dashboard on the driver's side near the door.

Air conditioning was a standard fitment on the XJ12. Its rev counter was calibrated to an impressive 7000rpm while the speedometer read to no less than 160mph. Lastly, a discreet gold-plated 'V12' badge appeared on the centre console just to let everyone know they were being propelled in something very special!

Externally the XJ12 used exactly the same shell

available in automatic form, using initially the Borg Warner Model 12 unit, later up-rated to the General Motors GM400 'box.

Inside, the XJ12 was very much as the XJ6 although subtle changes were made. These included Daimler-style door pulls, new-style front seat backs and a black Rexine finish to the centre console (instead of the

as the XJ6 but with minor trim changes. A new-style vertical-slatted radiator grille appeared, with a prominent central bar and a 'V12' badge at the top. At the rear the script 'XJ12' appeared at the bottom right-hand side of the boot panel. Along with the new style wheels, these were the only signs that this was not 'just' an XJ6.

The heart of the XJ12: the beautiful V12 four-carburettor engine which provided such phenomenal performance and yet such refinement. The penalty was an insatiable appetite for petrol.

At launch the XJ12 cost £3725, only a few hundred pounds dearer than its six-cylinder sister. A Daimler version called the Double Six was also available featuring the usual attributes of that marque.

Although released at a time of fuel crisis around the world, the XJ12 was very well received and not only won the Car of the Year Award but also had the distinction of being the fastest production saloon car in the world at that time.

DOUBLE SIX VANDEN PLAS

Known to have existed at the same time as the launch of the XJ12 in July 1972, Jaguar decided not to launch its up-market Vanden Plas version until September. Known as the Daimler Double Six Vanden Plas it retailed at the premium price of £5368. On the placement of an order, a standard V12 would be taken off the production line and transported to the Vanden Plas coachworks in London, whereupon it would be completely retrimmed in leather with bespoke seating, better quality carpeting and veneer and a distinct range of colour schemes complete with Everflex vinyl roof. Vanden Plas badging, a chromium trim swage line and standard fog/spot lights finished off an opulent specification.

The most important advance in the Vanden Plas, however, came in the longer-wheelbase bodyshell, which provided an extra four inches, all in the rear passenger compartment, resulting in extra legroom and longer rear doors.

LONG-WHEELBASE STANDARD SALOONS

Jaguar continued to develop the XJ range to keep pace with technology and the competition. The most significant of the Series 1 changes was the wider availability of the long-wheelbase bodyshell from the Vanden Plas. This occurred in October 1972, just one month after the announcement of the Vanden Plas, so it had obviously been agreed by the Jaguar management in advance.

The extra metal in the long-wheelbase cars added 1.5cwt to the overall weight, but this didn't seem to affect handling or performance significantly. The short-wheelbase cars (as they would henceforth be known) continued in production alongside the longer cars, which were offered at a few hundred pounds extra.

The Series 1 XJ saloons were a phenomenal success for Jaguar. Production reached over 98,000 examples of all models up to July 1973 when the models were replaced by the new Series 2 (discussed in the next chapter).

Accommodation for rear seat passengers was significantly improved in long-wheelbase versions (above). This advantage would prove decisive, as Jaguar standardised it on the Series 2 XJ. Compare the original short-wheelbase XJ (below left) with the long-wheelbase version (below right) which joined it in late 1972. An extra four inches were added behind the 'B' pillar, lengthening the rear doors and improving passenger space, but adding weight.

SPECIFICATIONS

XJ6/SOVEREIGN SERIES 1 (1968-73)

Engine: 2791cc/4235cc six-cylinder twin overhead camshaft
Bore & stroke: 83 × 86mm/92.07 × 106mm
Power output: 180bhp at 6000rpm/245bhp at 5500rpm
Transmission: Four-speed manual with or without over-drive, or Borg Warner three-speed automatic
Wheelbase: 9ft ¾in (276cm)/9ft 4¼in (286cm)
Length: 15ft 9½in (481cm)/16ft 2¾in (495cm) lwb
Width: 5ft 9in (175cm)
Height: 4ft 6in (137cm)
Weight: 32/33/34cwt (1626/1676/1727kg)
Suspension: Front: independent, semi-trailing double wishbones, coil springs, anti-roll bar. Rear: independent, lower wishbone/upper driveshaft link, radius arms, twin coil springs
Brakes: Girling four-wheel discs, vacuum assistance
Top speed: 117/124mph (187/198kmh)
0-50mph (80kmh): 8.2 secs/6.6 secs
Price New: £1897/£2258

XJ12/DOUBLE SIX SERIES 1 (1972-73)

As XJ6 except:
Engine: 5343cc V12-cylinder single overhead camshaft per bank
Bore & stroke: 90mm × 70mm
Power output: 253bhp at 6000rpm
Transmission: Automatic only
Weight: 35cwt (1778kg)
Top speed: 140mph (224kmh)
0-50mph (80kmh): 5.9 secs
Price new: £3725
Total Production:
XJ6 2.8-litre 19,322; XJ6 4.2-litre swb 59,077; XJ6 4.2-litre lwb 874; XJ12 swb 2474; XJ12 lwb 754; Sovereign 2.8-litre 3233; Sovereign 4.2-litre swb 11522; Sovereign 4.2-litre lwb 386; Double-Six swb 534; Double-Six Vanden Plas 351
Grand Total 98,527

CHAPTER TWENTY

XJ SERIES 2

1973-79

Restyling features of the XJ Series 2 were raised bumpers, a shorter
front grille, reshaped wings and revised trim. The 4.2-litre version
unfortunately had reduced power compared with the Series 1.

The top-of-the-range Daimler Double Six Vanden Plas continued in Series 2 form, seen here with
Kent alloy wheels. A 4.2-litre Vanden Plas also joined it.

Even though the Series 1 XJ was exceptionally
successful, there were criticisms and a need to
update the models to meet ever more stringent
regulations, particularly for North America. So Jaguar
introduced the brand new Series 2 XJ at the Frankfurt
Motor Show in August 1973.

The range of saloons now consisted of 4.2- and 5.3-
litre engined models in both Jaguar and Daimler forms
as well as the luxurious Vanden Plas version. Gone,
however, were the 2.8-litre engined cars, although they
were listed as production models at the very outset.
Significant newcomers during the life of the Series 2
were the two-door variants known as the XJ6C and
XJ5.3C, more commonly called the Coupé. Although
they were listed at launch in 1973, the Coupés did not
actually become available until April 1975 due to
development and production difficulties.

Mechanically the new model was very similar to the

The XJ12 continued with the same body revisions as the XJ6 and, as before, it had wider tyres and a 'V' on the grille.

outgoing Series 1, particularly in V12 form; the 4.2-litre six-cylinder cars performed less well as a result of a reduction in power to 170bhp at 4500rpm caused by the fitment of an American-style exhaust-heated air intake system to meet emission requirements. Also the Series 2 engines received a new type of oil cooler and solid exhaust downpipes merging into a double-skinned single pipe leading to separate silencers and tailpipes. All XJs were now fitted with ventilated front disc brakes and an electrically controlled battery cooling fan.

Structurally the Series 2 bodyshell was re-engineered, with side impact bars to the doors and a new single-skinned bulkhead assembly with asbestos lining on the engine side plus felt-and-bitumen for the passenger compartment to reduce noise levels. Further, all connections from the engine to the passenger compartment passed through multi-plug adaptors or solid piping, eliminating the need for drilled holes, rubber grommets and so on. Exterior changes had to take place to satisfy safety standards abroad. North American law demanded that bumper heights be raised to the specified 16in and this meant a re-design of the XJ's front end, with a reduced depth grille, a more prominent chromium-plated under-grille, a revised bumper and new under-riders. In turn this meant new

side/indicator lighting, now made entirely of plastic. At the rear the style remained unchanged save for a more prominent chromium boot-lid casting with built-in legislation-friendly number plate lighting.

All Series 2 cars featured ventilated disc wheels, in either paint finish or chromium plate depending on model and owner requirements. North American 'Federal' models featured side repeater lights on the front and rear wings along with rubber facings on the bumpers.

Internally the Series 2 XJ received even more attention to detail starting with the dashboard, still veneered but now of completely new design, with both the two main instruments *and* auxiliary gauges sited directly in front of the driver. Ergonomics were improved with the elimination of the confusing bank of identical switches, replaced by column stalk operation for wipers, washers, dip-switch, etc. The main lighting switch was now a knob below the instrument panel, flanking the steering column with its integral key ignition/starter switch.

The rest of the dashboard was taken up with an enlarged passenger glove box, new-style rectangular face-level air vents, a massive centrally situated air grille for the heater and/or air conditioning unit and below that a novel oddments tray connecting the dash-

Again there were both Jaguar and Daimler versions of most models in the range, and again the Daimler's grille (left) looked more elegant than the Jaguar's.

The dashboard was completely revised for the Series 2, notably with repositioned instruments and switchgear, and there was a new steering wheel.

For the first couple of years Series 2 production was carried out on the same line as E-types. Build quality was a cause for concern on the Series 2.

board to the centre console.

The console itself now incorporated the electric clock and four auxiliary switches for functions such as interior lighting and fuel tank changeover, below which were the radio panel and heater/air conditioning controls. A new two-spoke steering wheel with centre padding was fitted but the under-dashboard parcel shelves were deleted.

Peculiar to the Series 2 was the adoption of a fibre-optic lighting unit for switchgear and the standardisation of electric windows for all but the basic short-wheelbase six-cylinder models. New style seating, door panels and grab handles also made the Series 2 cars look different to their earlier counterparts and, as ever, slightly different trim was fitted to the Daimler derivatives.

A brand new body style in 1975 was the two-door Coupé, based on a short-wheelbase floorpan and featuring pillarless side glass. This is a 4.2-litre Daimler version with standard wheels.

The heater/ventilation and air conditioning systems were again totally redesigned for better efficiency in the Series 2 cars. As well as a more efficient and powerful heater unit, the system operated via a series of servo motors electrically controlled to provide small and instant changes in temperature upon request. The system was also geared thermostatically to maintain pre-set temperatures. The air conditioning unit, where fitted, was also substantially upgraded to meet the demands of hot countries.

The Series 2 saloons were available in both wheelbase lengths and started at a modest £3674 for the manual transmission 4.2-litre ranging up to £4702 for the long-wheelbase V12.

XJ COUPÉS (1975-77)

On introduction in 1975 the 4.2 and 5.3 two-door Coupé models were particularly well received as more exclusive members of the XJ range. Using a normal short-wheelbase floorpan plus front and rear ends and roof section, the Coupés adopted a pillarless two-door style. The doors were substantially heavier and four inches longer than the standard saloon's and, because of the lack of centre B-pillar, the frameless door windows (which had no quarterlights) and the rear windows could be wound down completely out of sight.

All production Coupés had a black vinyl roof covering and badging on the rear featured the 'C' insignia. Just as with the saloons, Daimler versions were also available. There was a slight loss in rear compartment leg room and of course there were tip-forward front seats to allow access to the rear passenger area.

Coupés were never as rigid as the saloons and in fact weighed less than both the Series 1 and 2 four-door models. Constant complaints were made about wind noise and water leaks on the Coupés which were never properly addressed. Along with production complications taking up valuable time and space required for saloon production, the Coupé became an inconvenience and died in November 1977 after a limited run of around 10,500 examples.

XJ 3.4-LITRE (1975-79)

In April 1975 a brand new smaller-engined version of the XJ saloon was released, effectively replacing the lost-cause 2.8-litre Series 1. Its 3442cc capacity was exactly the same as the old 3.4s of the 1950s and 1960s; however it utilised a strengthened version of the 4.2-litre block and the straight-port cylinder head. This meant that, when fitted with twin SU HS8 carburettors, the 3.4-litre unit developed 161bhp at 5000rpm, much the same as the original 3.4. It was available with a manual four-speed transmission or Borg Warmer's Model 65 automatic gearbox.

The 3.4-litre was never offered in the two-door Coupé bodyshell or as an upmarket Vanden Plas saloon but was strategically targeted at the management 'fleet' market. It had downgraded trim and was offered in both Jaguar and Daimler variants. Stain resistant cloth-trimmed seats replaced leather, but in a limited number of only five colours; and wind-up windows were the norm with no exterior swage coachline.

The 3.4-litre XJ6 was competitively priced at £4794, which was over £350 cheaper than the cheapest 4.2-litre XJ6. Of course performance was reduced (0-50mph in 7.8 seconds and as slow as 9.2 in automatic form with a maximum speed of 117mph). Moreover the saving in fuel consumption was marginal. 3.4-litre models were never as popular as Jaguar had hoped and only around 9000 examples were produced up to 1979.

All short-wheelbase four-door XJ saloons were discontinued in November 1974 and, although listed in the beginning, were never actually available in V12 form. The V12 models benefited from the addition of Lucas fuel injection from April 1975 which slightly improved fuel economy but boosted power to 285bhp.

The Coupé was an exciting new model which only ever appeared in Series 2 form. Although it was lighter and better performing, rigidity and weather sealing were perennial problems.

Another new Series 2 variant appeared later in production based on the top-of-the-range Daimler Vanden Plas, although this time with the 4.2-litre six-cylinder XK engine. Mechanically identical to the Daimler Sovereign but with Double Six Vanden Plas trim, the main advantage of the 4.2-litre version was improved fuel consumption.

Production of the Series 2 continued until February 1979 when the model was replaced by the next generation XJ, the Series 3. Basically the Series 2 XJs were excellent cars employing many fine and technologically advanced features; they performed well and to many looked more attractive than the Series 1 (particularly in Coupé form). However, the Achilles' heel of the Series 2 models was build quality, which was brought about, many thought, by the subsuming of the Jaguar/Daimler company into the British Leyland organisation. Whatever the reasons, the point in question was that Jaguars were gaining a reputation for unreliability, suspect build quality and poor longevity, a reputation which they would find hard to cast off.

Jaguar XJ12C could be ordered with attractive optional Kent alloy wheels. All side windows could be wound down for a taste of fresh-air motoring and a vinyl roof was always standard.

The 3.4-litre model, launched to replace the 2.8, is identified by its lack of a coachline.

SPECIFICATIONS

XJ6/SOVEREIGN SERIES 2 2.8/3.4-LITRE (1973/1975-79)

Engine: 2791cc/3442cc six-cylinder twin overhead camshaft
Bore & stroke: 83 × 86mm/83 × 106mm
Power output: 180bhp at 6000rpm/161bhp at 5000rpm
Transmission: Four-speed all-synchromesh manual with or without overdrive, or Borg Warner three-speed automatic
Wheelbase: 9ft ⅞in (276cm)/9ft 4¾in (286cm) lwb
Length: 15ft 9½in (481cm)/16ft 2¾in (495cm) lwb
Width: 5ft 9¼in (176cm)
Height: 4ft 6in (137cm)
Weight: 32cwt (1626kg)
Suspension: Front: independent, semi-trailing double wishbones, coil springs, anti-roll bar. Rear: independent, lower wishbone/upper driveshaft link, radius arms, twin coil springs
Brakes: Girling four-wheel ventilated discs, power assistance
Top speed: 117mph (187kmh)
0-50mph (80kmh): 7.8 secs
Price new: £4795
Total Production: XJ6 2.8 170; XJ6 3.4 6990; Sovereign 3.4 2341; **Grand Total** 9391

XJ6/SOVEREIGN SERIES 2 4.2-LITRE (1973-79)

As 3.4-litre except:
Engine: 4235cc six-cylinder twin overhead camshaft
Bore & stroke: 92.7 × 106mm
Power output: 170bhp at 4500rpm
Weight: 34cwt (1727kg)/33cwt (1676kg) Coupé

Top speed: 125mph (200kmh)
0-50mph (80kmh): 7 secs
Price new: £3674
Total Production: XJ6 4.2 swb 12,147; Sovereign 4.2 swb 2435; XJ6 4.2 lwb 57,804; Sovereign 4.2 lwb 14,351; XJ6 4.2C 6487; Sovereign 4.2C 1677; **Grand Total:** 95,081

XJ12/DOUBLE SIX SERIES 2 5.3-LITRE (1973-79)

Engine: 5343cc V12-cylinder single overhead camshaft per bank
Bore & stroke: 90 × 70mm
Power output: 253bhp at 6000rpm/285bhp at 5750rpm
Transmission: General Motors Hydra-matic automatic
Wheelbase: 9ft 4¾in (286cm)
Length: 16ft 2¾in (495cm)
Width: 5ft 9¼in (176cm)
Height: 4ft 6in (137cm)
Weight: 35cwt (1778kg)
Suspension: Front: independent, semi-trailing double wishbones, coil springs, anti-roll bar. Rear: independent, lower wishbone/upper driveshaft link, radius arms, twin coil springs
Brakes: Girling four-wheel ventilated discs, power assistance
Top speed: 147mph (235kmh)
0-50mph (80kmh): 6 secs
Price new: £4702
Total Production: XJ12 lwb 16,010; Double Six lwb 2608 Double Six VDP lwb 1726; XJ5.3C 1855; Double Six Coupé 407 **Grand Total:** 22,606

CHAPTER TWENTY-ONE

XJ Series 3

1979-92

The Series 3 XJ saloons were the final development of the original XJ line, representing a massive £7 million investment by Jaguar in what was essentially an 'interim' model prior to the launch of an all-new saloon, code-named XJ40. No-one (least of all Jaguar) could have forseen that the Series 3 would go on for another 13 years in production and would still, even today, be regarded as one of its finest ever models.

Launched to the public in March 1979, the Series 3 bodyshell was significantly redesigned. For the first time in its history Jaguar went outside its own styling department and chose the well respected Italian design house Pininfarina to rejuvenate the XJ. The brief was to retain as much of the basic design concept as possible but at the same time to provide the car with a new lease of life until the launch of its all-new replacement.

The most noticeable aspect of the redesign was the raising of the roofline to provide more interior space and larger window areas. The angles of the windscreen and rear window were inclined more to the vertical to achieve the extra height. Both were heat sealed into position to provide extra torsional strength to the bodyshell as a whole.

Minor changes affected most of the body panels including reshaped wheelarches, rear lighting, and bumpers with energy absorbing pistons, rubber surrounds and chromium-plated tops. The front bumper now incorporated the indicators and number plate while the side lights were contained within the outer headlight units. At the rear, the bumper incorporated twin rear foglamps, and new chrome trim around the boot lid brought a new look to the rear end. Returning to the front, another redesign of the radiator grille took place and extra indicator lights were placed on the front wings.

Another move forward for the Series 3 XJ was the fitment of new style flush-mounted pull door handles and the elimination of quarter lights from the front windows. The characteristically kicked-up leading edge of the rear wing had also been smoothed out.

Pininfarina redesigned the XJ to create the Series 3 in 1979. A higher roofline with more vertical front and rear screens gave a greater window area, and a new front grille and a smoothed-out 'kick' in the rear wing were other features.

The Series 3 (left) was significantly redesigned inside. Better seats, a new steering wheel, revised door trims and improved equipment distinguished the new model, although the dash remained broadly the same.
The entry-level 3.4-litre XJ6 (right) had plain wool blend tweed upholstery and straight grain woodwork.

The base 3.4-litre engine had twin carburettors, as on the Series 2, and produced 20bhp less than the Series 1 2.8-litre.

A new fuel injection system replaced carburettors on the 4.2-litre engine, boosting power to 200bhp.

Rubber-faced bumpers, reshaped wheelarches, and flush door handles were detail changes on the Series 3 XJ, which in 1979 was still sold through British Leyland dealerships.

Wheels were of the same size but of a new design and fitted as standard with novel stainless steel trims. Alternatively Kent alloy wheels could be specified as a cost option (carried over from some of the Series 2s and Vanden Plas models).

The Series 3 cabin was significantly improved over the previous models. The seats were redesigned and the seat backs were enlarged and now had a lumbar support adjustment as standard for both front occupants. Electric seat movement was a popular cost option and standard on the Vanden Plas.

Inertia reel seat belt mechanisms were now hidden within the trim panels and an electric sunroof panel became a cost option for all models except the Vanden Plas, on which it was standard. Another option was a headlamp wash/wipe system operated from the steer-

To many, the Pininfarina-designed Series 3's higher roof and bigger glasshouse made it the prettiest of all XJs.

ing column (again another standard fitment on Vanden Plas models).

A new design for the steering wheel, minor amendments to the style of instrumentation, warning lights and general dashboard area also helped to distinguish the new cars. Door trim panels changed, more luxurious carpeting was fitted and the steering column stalks changed positions to meet current European standards.

The enhanced specification of the Series 3 shone through with improved radio/stereo equipment, an electrically operated radio aerial that raised and lowered when the set was turned on and off, tinted windows for all models, courtesy light delay, improved centralised locking, halogen headlights, better sound deadening and the availability of cruise control (yet another standard fitment on the Vanden Plas). The boot even had a tool kit enclosed within a special brief-case and better carpeting.

The Series 3 XJ was released right from the start with a full range of engine options: 3.4, 4.2 and 5.3 litres. The 3.4-litre engine remained carburetted but the 4.2-litre gained fuel injection and OPUS electronic ignition, delivering over 200bhp for a significant boost in performance: 0-60mph in 10.5 seconds and an improved maximum speed of 128mph. Six-cylinder engines were also made quieter and more fuel efficient. By this time Jaguar had ceased production of its own manual transmission so, for the Series 3 six-cylinder cars, a strengthened version of the Rover SD1 five-speed gearbox was used.

Upon launch the Series 3 was available from a base price of just over £11,000 for the 3.4-litre to over £17,000 for the Vanden Plas.

Upgrades were carried out on all Series 3 XJs over the coming years, the first of which came in 1981 when the V12, which had consistently been an unreformed 'gas guzzler', received a newly designed May 'Fireball' cylinder head. Using a two-chamber combustion arrangement with the inlet valve recessed and the exhaust valve set higher so that the spark plug projected into it, a swirl action induced the mixture to be pushed by the piston from the inlet area to the combustion chamber on one stroke and this concentrated charge around the plug, enabling more rapid burning of a lean mixture.

The new system would be identified on subsequent V12 XJs as the 'HE' (for High Efficiency). It cost

The fuel-injected V12 engine – with new 'HE' heads from 1981 – under the S3 bonnet.

Later Jaguar XJs were fitted with stylish 'pepperpot' alloy wheels and were renamed Sovereign.

Jaguar several million pounds to develop and instantly proved its worth by improving the abysmal fuel consumption from around 12 to 14mpg and, on a run, up to 19 to 21mpg. Subsequently the V12s received a brand new General Motors GM400 automatic gearbox while the six-cylinder cars benefited from the fitment of the Borg Warner Model 66 unit.

In 1983 two significant changes took place in the marketing strategy of the XJ. Firstly Jaguar lost the right to use the Vanden Plas insignia on its home market models. By this time the finishing of these models had already been moved from London to Jaguar's own Browns Lane assembly plant, and from 1983 the Daimler versions would simply be known as Double Six, although continuing the superiority of trim over the Jaguar equivalents.

Later in that year, however, Jaguar made a decision to discontinue the Daimler models from most export markets and instead to launch a fully equipped up-market version of the Jaguar, taking over the Sovereign name from Daimler. This model was offered in both 4.2 and 5.3-litre guises and carried all the usual extra-cost options such as cruise control, air conditioning, headlamp wash/wipe and electric seats while also boasting a brand new 'pepperpot' style of alloy wheel. Now the only difference for the Daimler was the fitment of individual rear seats, fluted exterior brightwork, badging and full (instead of half) leather trim.

Minor trim changes continued through to 1985 by

The XJ12 continued in Series 3 form, identified by its wider tyres (here on Kent alloy wheels) and badging. Note the headlamp wipers. This is a 1979 model.

which time, even though spy shots of the forthcoming XJ40 had become commonplace, the Series 3 was selling better than ever, mainly due to improved build quality and competitive pricing. This was confirmed by the famed JD Power survey in America on customer satisfaction, in which Jaguar was rated fifth.

The 3.4-litre model received a trim revision in 1985 with new tweed upholstery, inset wood veneer for the door cappings and a straight-grain walnut dashboard panel. The larger engined cars also received minor trim upgrades.

Series 3s continued in full-scale production until the introduction of the XJ40 replacement in October 1986. The six-cylinder Series 3s finally left production in April 1987 yet the V12 cars continued on a limited run basis, literally made to order, way past their sell-by

The Vanden Plas name continued on Daimlers until 1983, always with leather upholstery, individual rear seating and inlaid woodwork.

date. This was for two reasons: firstly because there was still a demand for the model and secondly because Jaguar had not yet fully developed a V12-engined version of the XJ40.

The very last Jaguar V12 Sovereign left the production line in November 1991, while the Daimler Double Six soldiered on even further until November 1992 when the last of the Series 3 bodyshells finally ran out.

A grand total of 177,000 Series 3 XJs were produced from 1979 to 1992, another record for Jaguar. In total an amazing 402,848 XJs of all series had been made since 1968, making this the most prolific Jaguar ever. It is also perhaps a further tribute to the original XJ Series that the very latest X-300 models marked a return to the subtle styling themes which made the first XJ such a classic.

After the six-cylinder XJs were replaced by the XJ40 in 1986, the V12-engined Series 3 remained in production. Pictured are the Jaguar Sovereign (left) and Daimler Double Six (right).

SPECIFICATIONS

XJ6 SERIES 3 3.4-LITRE (1979-87)

Engine: 3442cc six-cylinder twin overhead camshaft
Bore & stroke: 83 × 106mm
Power output: 161bhp at 5000rpm
Transmission: Borg Warner three-speed automatic
Wheelbase: 9ft 4¾in (286cm)
Length: 16ft 2¾in (495cm)
Width: 5ft 9¼in (176cm)
Height: 4ft 6in (137cm)
Weight: 34cwt (1676kg)
Suspension: Front: independent, semi-trailing double wish-bones, coil springs, anti-roll bar. Rear: independent, lower wishbone/upper driveshaft link, radius arms, twin coil springs
Brakes: Girling four-wheel discs, power assistance
Top speed: 116mph (186kmh)
0-50mph (80kmh): 8 secs
Price new: £11,189
Total Production: 3.4-litre 5799

XJ6/SOVERIGN SERIES 3 4.2-LITRE (1979-87)

As 3.4-litre except:
Engine: 4235cc six-cylinder twin overhead camshaft
Bore & stroke: 92.07 × 106mm
Power output: 200bhp at 5000rpm
Transmission: Five-speed manual or Borg Warner three-speed automatic

Weight: 35½cwt (1803kg)
Brakes: Ventilated discs
Top speed: 128mph (205kmh)
0-50mph (80kmh): 7.7 secs
Price new: £12,326
Total Production:
XJ6 4.2 97,349; Jaguar Soverign 4.2 27,261;
Daimler Sovereign 4.2 20,315;
Daimler Sovereign VDP 4.2 1953; **Grand Total** 146,878

XJ12/DOUBLE SIX SERIES 3 5.3-LITRE (1979-92)

As 4.2-litre except:
Engine: 5343cc V12-cylinder single overhead camshaft per bank
Bore & stroke: 90 × 70mm
Power output: 285bhp at 5750rpm
Transmission: General Motors GM400 automatic
Weight: 37cwt (1880kg)
Top speed: 148mph (237kmh)
0-50mph (80kmh): 5.9 secs
Price new: £15,016
Total Production:
XJ12 5408; Jaguar Sovereign 5.3 9129; Double Six 9628;
Double Six VDP 401
Grand Total 24,566

CHAPTER TWENTY-TWO

XJS

1975-96

As related in an earlier chapter, the demise of the E-type and of Jaguar's sports car heritage was inevitable. With ever increasing regulations being thrust upon car manufacturers by North American Federal laws, it was thought at the time that this would be the nemesis of the true two-seater convertible. Jaguar set its sights on a replacement which would be seen as a much more sophisticated, refined and capable Grand Touring car.

To keep development costs to the minimum, it was decided that the new car, the XJS, would be built around the short wheelbase XJ saloon floorpan because the floorpan itself is probably the most expensive aspect of any new car. This floorpan was shortened further by some six inches, bringing the rear suspension closer to the centre of the car. With adjustments to the angle of the windscreen and bulkhead, better passenger accommodation was made available for what was effectively a more compact XJ. With

extra strengthening at the front the whole structure was nearly 100lb lighter than the equivalent XJ.

The brand new two-door 2+2 body had decidedly controversial styling. The usual Jaguar traditions of chrome, veneer and gentle curves had given way to matt black and transatlantic flatness! Apart from the Jaguar badging on the boot lid, there was nothing to indicate that this was a Jaguar at all: no chromed slatted grille, twin headlights instead of quads, no leaping mascot or even plated window frames. Instead at the front there was a rather nondescript grille aperture typical of the 1970s, one-piece rectangular light units and a full-width all-rubber impact absorbing bumper plus matching under-valance spoiler.

The sides were uncompromisingly slab-sided without even a swage line to break them up and the doors were wide with flush-fitting handles and matt black window surrounds. Perhaps the most controversial aspect of all, however, were the 'flying buttresses' at the

The XJS's controversial styling was more a product of the 1970s than an evolution of Jaguar themes, but its V12 engine and brilliant handling made it a fabulous grand tourer. Some magazines even called it 'the best car in the world'.

The XJS interior represented a distinct change for Jaguar, with much use of black plastic. Scalloped gauges sat astride rotating drum minor dials and a bank of warning lights.

rear. The rather flat roofline swept rearward at each side of the small rear screen, flowing down into the rear wings. Many critics dismissed them as failed ornaments but these 'fins' were in fact very aerodynamic and helped the car cope with strong cross-winds.

Large rear lights were placed on the extremities of the rear wings, following their shape, and there was a less formal number plate housing incorporating the 'Jaguar' name and reversing lights. Regardless of exterior paint finish, the rear edge of the boot lid was always painted matt black and there was a full-width rubber bumper.

The 285bhp V12 engine delivered performance in the supercar league, with a quoted top speed of well above 150mph and 0-60mph in under 7sec.

Nearly £6 million was invested in the XJS which, it was thought, would boost Jaguar's sales in that all-important North American market. Controversy, however, followed the car from the start. Most either loved or hated it at first sight, while the gut reaction to the interior could be equally extreme.

The complete lack of any signs of veneer or wood-work at all was a bold break for Jaguar. Instead matt black and aluminium was the order of the day. The XJS should have been a true four-seater but rear seat legroom was marginal to say the least, even with all-new slim-line leather seating, and a seating position low in the chassis. New wide-opening doors featured all-new trim, and the predominantly black dashboard, though incorporating a similar style centre console to the XJ Series, had a brand new instrument binnacle in front of the driver, the two main instruments sited either side of a 'bar' of minor gauges and a maze of warning lights above. Minor switching, handles, trim, steering wheel and so on came straight from the XJ parts bin.

The boot area was fully carpeted and contained an upright mounted spare wheel ahead of the 20-gallon

A shock for Jaguar traditionalists: the XJS had full rubber bumpers, a bland grille and ellipsoid headlamps. Greatest XJS controversy surrounded the 'flying buttress' rear design (below) leading to accusations of 'styling by committee'. They did at least help lateral stability.

fuel tank which, for Federal reasons, was situated across the rear seat area above the suspension. The battery was now boot-mounted and although this and the spare took up considerable room, overall luggage space was not too bad for a 2+2 grand tourer thanks to a lowered boot floor.

Mechanically the XJS was only available with the 5.3-litre V12 engine complete with fuel injection and either the Borg Warner Model 12 automatic transmission or Jaguar's own four-speed all-synchromesh gearbox. Suspension and brakes were carried over from the V12 saloon except for minor amendments to allow for the XJS's 2cwt lighter shell. Alloy wheels were featured as standard equipment.

The XJS was well equipped by any standards and was certainly a match for competitors like the Mercedes SL, Jensen and Ford Mustang. Included as standard were such items as air conditioning, electric windows and inertia reel seatbelts.

The XJS was never intended as a replacement for the E-type but was aimed at fulfilling the requirements of the sports/GT market during the coming decade. At a price of £8900 in 1975, the car was not cheap but it did offer exceptionally refined high performance motoring for the driver who didn't need a full four-seater and had outgrown the noisy, draughty sports car image.

The XJS was just about as fast as you could then get

Not a splinter of wood to be found in the matt black and anodised alloy interior. The manual gearbox was a rare choice, most customers opting for automatic.

Another criticism of the XJS was that rear seat accommodation was distinctly cramped for a car of its size, but at least it looked luxurious.

in a standard production 2+2, with a top speed in excess of 150mph and incredible acceleration times: the standing quarter mile in 15 seconds and 0-50mph in just over 5 seconds. Economy was not its strong point: single figures were to be expected if the performance was used. This rather pulled the carpet from under Jaguar's feet in its attempts to promote the XJS as Grand Touring transport since the 20-gallon fuel tank would need replenishing every 200 miles!

As with the V12 saloons, the XJS gained the more refined GM 400 automatic gearbox in 1977 and, by 1979, the manual transmission version had disappeared from the model listings. Eventually in 1981 the XJS received the 'HE' suffix, utilising the May Fireball

head already seen in the saloons, which improved its abysmal fuel consumption and boosted power output to 300bhp at 5400rpm.

To coincide with the introduction of the 'HE' engine, Jaguar, now under the leadership of John Egan, adopted a more traditional approach to the XJS's appearance. It gained chromed upper bumper covers over new style rubber bumpers (*à la* Series 3 saloons), a twin coachline along the body sides, side indicator repeaters, minor trim changes at the rear and new 'Starfish' alloy wheels unique to the XJS. These 6½in wide wheels now carried new Dunlop D7 tyres.

Internally the XJS was much improved by the adoption of real wood, not the usual walnut but elm of a

After 1981 the XJS received an 'HE' badge to denote its 'High Efficiency' engine, and new 'Starfish' alloy wheels and chrome-faced bumpers arrived at the same time. This is a US-spec car with four circular headlamps.

From the HE, all XJSs adopted wood veneer trim, nearly always in light burr elm rather than walnut. A trip computer is prominent in the centre of the dash. The Cabriolet (below) arrived in 1983, at first only with the new 3.6-litre AJ6 engine. It was not a full convertible, having rigid targa panels and a rear roof section which folded down.

very light hue. This featured on the dashboard, centre console switch plate and door cappings. New all-leather door trims and console were to be a standard feature on the XJS along with door lights and a Series 3 style leather rimmed steering wheel.

While the HE gave the XJS a new lease of life for the 1980s, lifting sales considerably, it could be said that Jaguar had missed the opportunity to market a smaller six-cylinder engined version. At this time, in 1983, the development of a brand new AJ6 engine for the planned XJ40 saloon was coming to a conclusion and, just as the XK engine had been tried and tested in the XK120 sports in 1948 and the 5.3-litre V12 had been initially launched in the E-type, so it was that Jaguar took the opportunity to announce the new AJ6 power unit in its sports/GT car before the launch of the new saloon.

Full details of the new power unit appear in the next chapter on the XJ40 models. Suffice it to say that, as fitted to the XJS from September 1983 to provide a sis-

The XJR-S was a special model developed with TWR in 1988. Colour coded bumpers, a front air dam, side skirts, 15in Speedline alloy wheels, a rear apron and boot spoiler distinguish it.

ter model to the V12, the new engine was an in-line six-cylinder, multi-valve, overhead camshaft unit of 3.6 litres capacity with Lucas/Bosch fuel injection. The new engine developed 225bhp at 5300rpm and was significantly lighter than both the old XK unit and the V12.

Arriving on the scene only in manual transmission form using a brand new German Getrag five-speed gearbox, the smaller engined XJS was certainly no sluggard. Although slower than its big brother, the 3.6-litre XJS performed well, even if you had to keep the revs up to get the most out of the engine. 0-50mph came up in 5.6 seconds with 100mph arriving in 19.7, plus a maximum speed of 141mph. Fuel consumption was one of the big advantages behind the new XJS: using the performance to the full, a low of 16 to 17mpg might be achieved or, driven with care, you could get over 25mpg.

The XJS 3.6-litre was launched in August 1983 at £19,289, about £3000 cheaper than the V12. Apart from the engine/gearbox, the only other mechanical changes included the removal of the rear anti-roll bar, a reduction in size of the front anti-roll bar, and softer spring ratings as the car was slightly lighter than the V12 version.

At the same time as Jaguar launched the 3.6-litre

fixed head, it also introduced another new XJS, the Cabriolet. Jaguar had not produced a convertible since the demise of the E-type in 1975, although outside specialists had converted Jaguar saloons and even XJSs to convertibles to customer order.

Under the John Egan regime it was considered prudent to bring out a 'ragtop' XJS to satisfy the many requests for such a car from the general public, especially in the North American market. Federal bureaucracy never did outlaw convertibles, which were in fact coming back into fashion.

The Cabriolet did not have its own separate shell. Instead Jaguar released standard fixed heads to an outside contractor which cut off the roof and rear buttresses and welded in a new cross member to the floorpan, steel cant rails over the tops of the doors and a crossbar between the B-posts. The amended bodies were then sent back to Jaguar for painting and assembly whereupon they went on to Aston Martin's Tickford bodyworks for fitment of the hood and solid removable targa panels, roof trimming, etc. Later on in the life of the XJS Cabriolet, final assembly of the hood and so on was carried out at Jaguar's own Browns Lane plant due to problems with quality control at Tickford.

Internally, although basically similar to the fixed

head, the XJS Cabrio-
let had no rear seats,
simply a carpeted lug-
gage deck with rails
and lockable chests.
This was done as a
safety feature as, in
those days, it was not
a legal requirement to wear rear seat
belts and if, in the case of an accident, a
rear seat passenger was thrown upward
and forward, it might have been possible to get decapitated on the steel crossbar!

Cabriolets were, however, a little
more lavishly equipped than the fixed
heads as trim was 100 per cent leather
instead of part-leather. With the twin
targa panels in place and the rear hood
erect, the car was well insulated from
wind noise, looked attractive and had
inherent structural strength so as not to
suffer from the usual convertible malady of scuttle
shake.

*The Cabriolet was at first built by Tickford as a conversion of the standard XJS, but
from 1985, the year this targa-roofed model was fitted with the V12, Jaguar
assumed production itself at Browns Lane (above left). Coinciding with the
Cabriolet's launch, the XJS became the first Jaguar to use the AJ6 3.6-litre multi-
valve six-cylinder engine (above right). Very little was given away to the V12 in
terms of performance, but refinement was poor on early engines. The 3.6-litre XJSs
received another revised interior (below) with half leather/wool seating.*

The one major drawback to the Cabriolet was boot
space. An 'envelope' was provided for the storage of
the twin targa panels when removed from the roof,
which took up a sizeable amount of the already scant
luggage accommodation. Because the targa was a
design afterthought, if the panels were stored in a completely vertical position within the envelope, upon
closing the boot they could cause the boot lid to bend!

The Cabriolet could also be supplied with the extra-
cost option of a fitted hardtop for the rear hood section. This meant removing the existing hood but provided a more secure roof area and the fitment of a
heated glass rear window was of great benefit.

Initially the XJS Cabriolet was only released in 3.6-
litre manual form. However, in July 1985 a V12 ver-

sion came on the mar-
ket at £26,995, some
£3000 more than the
equivalent coupé. By
1987 both the 3.6-
litre Cabriolet and
coupé became avail-
able with a brand new
ZF four-speed automatic transmission
incorporating a 'Sport' mode.

From that year on, the XJS was consistently updated to keep abreast of the
competition in terms of luxury fitments
and trim. Heated door mirrors, heated
and electric lumbar support seats,
bright stainless steel sill plates, lattice-
type alloy wheels and revised walnut
veneer with extra wood trim on the
centre console all enhanced the XJS's
customer appeal. Later, sportier suspension was added and there were yet
more trim changes.

In 1988 Jaguar decided to drop the 3.6-litre Cabriolet model from the range and, at the end of that year,
the V12 Cabriolet also bit the dust. This left only the
coupés to hold the fort alongside a new sportier version called the XJR-S, developed by TWR, which had
successfully raced Jaguars on the company's behalf.
This more powerful version included a select range of
trim and exterior changes as well as a whole list of
suspension, brake and engine modifications to customer request.

Jaguar had, up to this time, also thought of producing other versions of the XJS including a long-wheelbase fixed head and a Daimler Double Six S, but nei-
ther came to fruition as production models.

Making its debut at the Geneva Motor Show in
March 1988 came the most striking XJS to date, the
'true' Convertible. Based on a revised bodyshell with

A full two-seater convertible superseded the Cabriolet in 1988. Fitted with an electrically-operated mohair top and available only with the V12 engine, it was the most elegant XJS yet but had taken 13 years to arrive.

The 1990 Le Mans V12 limited edition (of 280 cars) had sports suspension, 16in forged alloy wheels, full leather interior and four headlamps. At £38,700, this was the ultimate XJS coupé at the time.

significant stiffening, the two-seater, two-door car at last began to look like a cohesive design. An electric ram-operated mohair hood retracted and at the same time wound down the rear windows, and was unusual in that it featured an electrically heated glass rear window. The fully-lined hood and mechanism were a triumph of engineering when one considers that the basic shell derived from as long ago as 1975 and was never intended to be a convertible.

For the Convertible new frameless doors were used. Interior trim followed the top-of-the-range model and retained the same rear deck treatment as the Cabriolet. The Convertible featured a new mechanical development for Jaguar, the Teves ABS system, which was also used in the last of the Series 3 saloons. Launched only in V12 form, this flagship XJS sold for around £40,000 but was so eagerly sought after on release that premium prices were being asked for a considerable time until production matched sales requirements.

For 1991 Jaguar invested over £50 million in the XJS to give it yet another lease of life. Mechanically this meant adopting the 4.0-litre AJ6 engine to replace the 3.6 and the inclusion of a catalytic exhaust system. The new engine developed 223bhp despite the catalyst and could provide a 0-60mph time of 8.4 seconds in automatic form, with an improved top speed of over 140mph. Meanwhile the V12 received a new Marelli engine management system which reduced power by 5bhp to 280bhp.

Bodily, over 40 per cent of the shell was new although the car still retained its XJS look. New grille, headlights, glass area, frameless doors on the coupé, direct glazing for front and rear screens, new rear wings and rear end styling all helped to bring the XJS

a little more up-to-date, as indeed it needed to be since there was no model to replace it in the pipeline.

The interior received its first major re-vamp since 1975, including analogue instrumentation along with many other touches taken from the XJ40 saloons. There was sports-style seating (electrically operated), a new trip computer, restyled rear seating and many other improvements. Prices inevitably rose, the basic 4.0-litre coupé costing £33,400 in manual transmission form and the top-of-the-range V12 convertible weighing in at £50,600.

Within a year, the Convertible became available with the 4.0-litre engine as well and, for the 1994 model year, even more significant changes were made to keep the XJS competitive. The front and rear ends were again restyled with the addition of larger, wraparound bumpers finished in body colour, and there were new alloy wheels and slightly amended trim. Most important were the fitment of the brand new AJ16 power unit for the 4.0-litre model and the replacement of the old 5.3-litre engine by a new 6.0-litre V12 power plant. The AJ16 was destined for the new X-300 saloons (discussed in more detail in a later chapter) while the 6.0-litre was a new addition to the XJ40 saloon range from 1993.

The XJS has survived into 1996, Convertibles outselling coupés by a ratio of three-to-one. The model has consistently scored steady sales despite its advancing age. It is, to date, the longest-serving Jaguar model ever – although the V12 model has now gone out of production (except to special order). The remainder of the range will shortly be replaced by an all-new car which will carry the Jaguar sports/GT theme into the next century.

The XJS received a £50 million revamp in 1991, with extensive bodywork changes (rear wings, windows and full-width rear lights were the most significant) and a new 4.0-litre version of the AJ6 engine. From 1993 the Convertible (below) was offered with an enlarged 6.0-litre V12 and long-overdue 2+2 seating, prompted perhaps by Princess Diana's decision to buy a Mercedes convertible because it had rear seats.

These are the 1996 model year XJS models, dubbed 'Celebration' to commemorate 60 years of the Jaguar marque.

S P E C I F I C A T I O N S

XJS 5.3-LITRE (1975-93)

Engine: 5343cc V12-cylinder single overhead camshaft per bank
Bore & stroke: 90 × 70mm
Power output: 285bhp at 5500rpm/333bhp at 5250rpm XJR-S
Transmission: Four-speed manual (to 1981) or GM 400 three-speed automatic
Wheelbase: 8ft 6in (259cm)
Length: 15ft 11½in (486cm)
Width: 5ft 10½in (179cm)
Height: 4ft 1½in (126cm)
Weight: 33cwt (1676kg)
Suspension: Front: independent, wishbones, coil springs, anti-roll bar. Rear: independent, lower wishbone/upper driveshaft link, radius arms, coil springs, anti-roll bar
Brakes: Girling four-wheel ventilated discs, power assisted
Top speed: 153mph (245kmh)/158mph (253kmh) XJR-S
0-50mph (80kmh): 5.1 secs
Price new: £8900/£50,000XJR-S
Total Production: 5.3 Coupé manual 352; 5.3 Coupé auto 60,857; 5.3 XJR-S 448; 5.3 Cabriolet 3863; 5.3 Convertible 16,871
Grand Total 82,391

XJS 3.6-LITRE (1983-91)

As 5.3-litre except:
Engine: 3590cc six-cylinder multi-valve twin overhead camshaft
Bore & stroke: 91 × 92mm
Power output: 225bhp at 5300rpm
Transmission: Five-speed Getrag manual or three-speed automatic
Weight: 32cwt (1626kg)
Top speed: 141mph (226kmh)
0-50mph (80kmh): 5.6 secs

Price new: £19,289/£20,756
Total Production: 3.6 Coupé 8860; 3.6 Cabriolet 1146
Grand Total 10,006

XJS 4.0-LITRE (1991-96)

As 5.3-litre except:
Engine: 3980cc six-cylinder multi-valve twin overhead camshaft
Bore & stroke: 91 × 102mm
Power output: 223bhp at 4750rpm/238bhp at 4750rpm from 1994
Transmission: Five-speed Getrag or four-speed automatic with 'Sport' mode
Brakes: Electronic ABS and yaw control
Top speed: 142mph (227kmh)/147mph (235kmh) from 1994
0-50mph (80kmh): 6 secs/5.9 secs from 1994
Price new: £33,400
Total Production: 4.0 Coupé (to August 1995) 5392; 4.0 Convertible (to August 1995) 10,991
Grand Total (to August 1995) 16,383

XJS 6.0-LITRE (1993-95)

As 4.0-litre except:
Engine: 5994cc V12-cylinder single overhead camshaft per bank
Bore & stroke: 90 × 78.5mm
Power output: 318bhp at 5400rpm
Transmission: GM four-speed electronic automatic
Weight: 33cwt (1676kg)
Top speed: 155mph (248kmh)
0-50mph (80kmh): 6.1 secs
Price new: £55,000
Total Production: 6.0 Coupé (to August 1995) 772; 6.0 Convertible (to August 1995) 149; 6.0 XJR-S 389
Grand Total (to August 1995) 1310

CHAPTER TWENTY-THREE

XJ40

1986-94

The long-awaited new XJ6 arrived in 1986. The bottom-of-the-range model was the 2.9-litre which, with only 165bhp, was underpowered and was produced for only four years.

XJ40 was the code-name for the next generation of XJ saloons, which had been under development at Jaguar since the early 1970s yet only came to fruition towards the end of 1986. During that time significant developments took place to ensure better build quality and component reliability and to develop the design and technology befitting a Jaguar of the late 1980s and 1990s.

The XJ6 had gained a strong reputation over the years and so, despite the fact that the XJ40 was essentially a brand new model, Jaguar opted to retain the old model name XJ6. The new car's shape followed the maxim 'evolution not revolution' although its lines were generally more squared-up.

Launched only in six-cylinder form – the Series 3

XJ12 continued in production (see earlier chapter) – the new car was available either with the familiar 221bhp 3.6-litre AJ6 multi-valve power unit first seen in the XJS or a new 2.9-litre six-cylinder version with single camshaft developing a modest 165bhp at 5600rpm. Transmission was either via the Getrag five-speed manual gearbox (again as seen in the XJS) or a new four-speed ZF automatic transmission with a special 'J Gate' selector allowing a second plane of shift movement for instant gear changes, more suited to the sportier motorist.

The rear suspension was also new, with outboard disc brakes and lower wishbones which could move in a fore-and-aft direction to absorb force and prevent the transmission of noise and vibration. The differential was now also capable of absorbing vibration much better than before. Another innovation for Jaguar was the availability on top-of-the-range models of a self-levelling system on the rear suspension, using struts pressurised from an engine-driven pump with sensors and electronic control. The XJ40's front suspension followed that of the previous XJ series and ABS was also available on most models from the outset.

The XJ40's interior represented a total rethink although it did not abandon the traditional Jaguar saloon atmosphere. There was tweed upholstery for the lower models, partial leather for prestige Jaguar versions and full leather for Daimlers, pre-formed door panelling, new-style seats, some with full electronic movement, and new advanced heating and ventilation equipment (with or without a much more efficient air conditioning system according to model status).

The biggest change internally came in the dashboard. A brand new instrument pack incorporating the latest state-of-the-art technology appeared, a total break in tradition for Jaguar. Bar gauges replaced normal analogues, although the speedometer and tachometer remained of the normal circular type.

At the top end of the new XJ40 range was the Jaguar Sovereign 3.6 with its alloy wheels, chrome window frames and rectangular headlamps.

A much more modern approach to the later type XJ40 interior included plain instruments, more sophisticated electronics and better ergonomics. Note the J-gate automatic gear selector.

A large 'window' to the right of the instrument pack provided digital diagrams of all aspects of car management, indicating such problems as doors open, ABS brake failure, low oil pressure and so on, all of which were wired up to the on-board computer mounted on a pod below the instrument pack to the side of the steering wheel. The computer gave significantly more information than the units on previous Jaguars. The computer was also linked to a digital speedometer and

mileometer readout which could be altered to read imperial or metric units (and was built to beat the speedo clockers).

Externally, every body panel was new and the shell had been developed with new technology in mind, making for ease of panel replacement, better build quality on the assembly line and much better rust-proofing.

The overall appearance was much squarer than previous Jaguar saloons. A rather rectangular frontal aspect was evoked by the radiator grille and the halogen headlights on the top-of-the-range models (the standard saloons receiving four conventional headlights). The bumpers were of a similar style to the Series 3 but now incorporated side-mounted reflectors and a more prominent under valance spoiler to improve air flow. The bonnet and front wings were flatter and the centre section styling was similar to the Series 3 but with squarer panels, new-style door handles and either matt black or chrome surrounds to windows dependent on model. A larger front screen now sported a single wiper while the deeper rear screen helped to brighten the interior.

At the rear the familiar 'haunches' of the original XJ were still in evidence but the squared-up look was emphasised by a completely flat boot panel, new lighting treatment and a slimmer under-valance panel without protruding exhaust pipes. The new XJ6 had metric sized wheels and tyres, either with conventional steel rims and plastic rimbellishers or vaned alloys. The boot area was slightly improved with a greater depth, the spare wheel being mounted upright (*à la* XJS) and there was a new fitted toolkit.

Whether or not the XJ40 was a styling advance over the 18-year-old XJ6 is open to question. In plain 2.9-litre form with four headlamps the XJ40 perhaps looked its best.

The new XJ6 range consisted of a variety of models from a basic 2.9-litre manual saloon, strategically priced for the management fleet market at only £16,200, a 2.9-litre Sovereign providing the benefit of square halogen headlights, more brightwork, electrically operated seats, air conditioning, leather upholstery, cruise control, computer and so on to a 3.6-litre saloon, 3.6-litre Sovereign and of course the top-of-the-range Daimler models with unique rear seating, all-leather trim and fluted exterior brightwork.

The XJ40 could never be mistaken for any car but a Jaguar. This is one of the later base model 3.2-litre saloons with add-on wheel trims.

The new XJ40 provided an even better ride than any previous Jaguar. As well as improved comfort and specification it also had superior fuel economy: the 3.6-litre XJ6 could easily attain 25mpg on a run. Voted Car of the Year, Jaguar need not have worried about the XJ40's success, so vital to the continued growth of the company. In its first four years the XJ40 achieved record levels of sales and the model was continually developed and upgraded throughout its life, with items such as ABS becoming standard on most models.

It wasn't long before Jaguar's racing counterpart TWR under the name of JaguarSport offered its own sportier version of the XJ40 with modified trim, spoilers, uprated suspension and engines tuned to personal requirements, named the XJR6.

From 1990 the AJ6 engine was upgraded to 4.0 litres capacity by virtue of a stroke increased to 102mm, thereby increasing peak torque to 285lb ft at 3750 rpm, though power went up by only 2bhp. Reprofiled camshafts and valve timing, new pistons and a forged steel crankshaft improved engine refinement, while a new digital engine management system helped improve the 0-60mph time by 4 seconds and marginally boosted top speed. Accompanying the engine change, a new ZF four-speed electronic transmission interfaced with the engine management system, adding a 'Sport' mode for spirited driving.

A new ABS system and a much improved interior with conventional analogue instruments distinguished the new larger-engined XJ6 and, externally, more brightwork differentiated the top-of-the-range models.

Rear styling mirrored the front end's drift towards square edges, although the kicked-up rear wing remained as an echo of the original XJ.

The JaguarSport XJR 3.6 was the sports version of the XJ40, with suspension and engines tuned to customer requirements. Colour-coded body styling panels and special wheels marked the XJR apart.

A 4.0-litre version of the XJR naturally followed, now with a claimed maximum speed of over 150mph and 0-60mph in 6.7 seconds.

In October 1990 the 2.9-litre engine was also expanded, now up to 3.2 litres capacity and with twin overhead camshafts. It developed 200bhp, with speed and acceleration very similar to the old 3.6.

For 1993 new (non-metric) wheels and tyres were fitted along with a host of interior and exterior refinements. In the last couple of years of production, such items as driver and passenger air bags became standard equipment. Even bigger news for 1993 was the introduction in March of the much acclaimed V12 engined versions in both Jaguar and Daimler forms. Now of 6.0 litres capacity, the V12 boasted 318bhp, giving a 0-60mph time of 6.8 seconds and a maximum speed of 155mph, fine achievements considering the switch to unleaded fuel and catalytic converters. Equipped with a new General Motors automatic transmission linked to the engine management system

Expanded from 3.6 to 4.0 litres in 1990, the larger AJ6 engine developed only slightly more power but significantly more torque. A new engine management system improved performance by a very large margin.

This Daimler 4.0, as a top-of-the-range model, featured more brightwork.

When it finally arrived, the XJ12's 6.0 litres and 318bhp ensured that it was the fastest Jaguar saloon to date: 155mph and 0-60mph in 6.8 seconds were quoted.

and harder 'sports pack' suspension, the V12 was the ultimate XJ40.

During 1993 and 1994 Jaguar effectively ran down XJ40 production in readiness for the world launch of its next brand new saloon, code-named X-300. Jaguar had experienced a fall-off in world sales during the recession of the late 1980s and early 1990s, just like all other executive car manufacturers and, in a (successful) attempt to maintain interest in the 'old' car, it launched a range of special, one could almost say limited edition, saloons based on the XJ40.

For the latter half of 1993 this started with the introduction of the 3.2-

A special order long-wheelbase (with 5in added) conversion of the XJ40 was offered from 1993 under the names Majestic and Insignia. Prime Minister John Major was a celebrated customer.

litre S saloon, with a sportier character for the younger executive. This was also offered in 4.0-litre form for the 1994 model year. With different upholstery, a rosewood veneer internal finish, sports pack suspension, alloy wheels, colour-coded mirrors and inset rear boot panel, the 3.2 S offered a high degree of prestige at a price below £30,000.

During the last 18 months of XJ40 production other models were amended in specification to enhance their differentiation within the range. In March 1994 a new base model, the XJ6 Gold, came on the scene. For an incredibly low price of only £28,950, the Gold offered

Top of the range in 1992 was the Daimler 4.0 24V with its standard fog lamps, airbag, individual rear seats and extra brightwork.

The 6.0-litre V12 Daimler and Jaguar arrived in 1993. Undoubtedly great cars, their life was fleeting. The V12 was the rarest engine in any XJ40, only 3799 of all types being delivered.

a bespoke if limited range of exterior colour schemes, triple-pleat piped leather upholstery, automatic transmission, burr walnut veneer, extra leather trim on items like the handbrake lever, colour-keyed door trims and dashboard top rail, Kiwi alloy wheels and of course 'Gold' badging. The car was a major boost to sales, helping Jaguar to clear out stocks of XJ40 bodyshells during this crucial period.

At the time of the launch of the X-300, XJ40 prices were still very competitive, from the excellent value

Gold to the £56,200 top-of-the-range Daimler Double Six equipped with literally everything one could want, including such extravagances as an automatic electronic dipping rear view mirror and door mirrors that swivelled to show the pavement whenever reverse gear was selected!

Although only in production for some eight years, the XJ40 moved Jaguar further forward in the luxury car sector and a grand total of 208,672 models were produced.

Trim levels improved as the years went by. This 1993 XJ12 (left) boasts inlaid woodwork, electric seats and all-analogue gauges. Walnut picnic tables and individual rear seats (right) continued decades of tradition in the Daimler Double Six.

SPECIFICATIONS

XJ6 2.9-LITRE (1986-90)

Engine: 2919cc six-cylinder single overhead camshaft multi-valve
Bore & stroke: 91 × 74.8mm
Power output: 165bhp at 5600rpm
Transmission: Five-speed Getrag manual or four-speed automatic with J-gate selector
Wheelbase: 9ft 5in (287cm)
Length: 16ft 4½in (499cm)
Width: 6ft 6¾in (200cm)
Height: 4ft 6½in (138cm)
Weight: 32¾cwt (1664kg)
Suspension: Front: independent, unequal length double wishbones, coil springs, anti-roll bar. Rear: independent, lower wishbone/upper driveshaft link, single coil spring, damper
Brakes: Four-wheel ventilated discs, outboard rear, power assistance
Top speed: 117mph (187kmh)
0-50mph (80kmh): 7 secs
Price new: £16,200
Total Production: 14,148

XJ6 3.6-LITRE (1986-91)

As XJ6 2.9-litre except:
Engine: 3590cc six-cylinder twin overhead camshaft multi-valve
Bore & stroke: 91 × 92mm
Power output: 221bhp at 5000rpm
Weight: 33cwt (1676kg)
Top speed: 137mph (219kmh)
0-50mph (80kmh): 5.5 secs
Price new: £18,495
Total Production: Daimler 3.6 10,314; Jaguar 3.6 9349; Jaguar Sovereign 3.6 50,291; Federal 3.6 13,319
Grand Total 83,273

XJ6 3.2-LITRE (1991-94)

As XJ6 2.9-litre except:
Engine: 3239cc six-cylinder twin overhead camshaft multi-valve

Bore & stroke: 91 × 83mm
Power output: 200bhp at 5250rpm
Weight: 33cwt (1676kg)
Top speed: 132mph (211kmh)
0-50mph (80kmh): 6.1 secs
Price new: £29,950
Total Production: Jaguar/Daimler 3.2 13,053; Sport 3.2 3117; Jaguar Sovereign 3.2 3487; Gold 3.2 1499
Grand Total 21,156

XJ6 4.0-LITRE (1991-94)

As XJ6 2.9-litre except:
Engine: 3980cc six-cylinder twin overhead camshaft multi-valve
Bore & stroke: 91 × 102mm
Power output: 223bhp at 4750rpm/248bhp XJR
Weight: 33cwt (1676kg)
Top speed: 138mph (221kmh)
0-50mph (80kmh): 5 secs
Price new: £44,000
Total Production: Jaguar 4.0 13,576; Daimler 4.0 8876; Jaguar Sovereign 4.0 50,336; Federal 4.0 12,846; Sport 4.0 500; Gold 4.0 23; Long Wheelbase 4.0 121
Grand Total 86,296

XJ12 6.0-LITRE (1993-94)

As XJ6 2.9-litre except:
Engine: 5994cc V12-cylinder single overhead camshaft per bank
Bore & stroke: 90 × 78.5mm
Power output: 318bhp at 5400rpm
Transmission: Four-speed electronic GM automatic transmission only
Weight: 34cwt (1727kg)
Brakes: With ABS and yaw control
Top speed: 155mph (248kmh)
0-50mph (80kmh): 5.2 secs
Price new: £60,000
Total Production: Jaguar Sovereign 6.0 1243; Daimler Double Six 985; Jaguar (export) 6.0 1521; Long Wheelbase 6.0 50 **Grand Total** 3799

CHAPTER TWENTY-FOUR

JAGUAR X-300

1994 TO DATE

The starring role in the range of models at launch went to the sensational supercharged XJR, distinguished by its wire-mesh grille and chunky alloy wheels.

Although the XJ40 saloons had carried Jaguar successfully through eight turbulent years as a continuing producer of quality luxury motorcars with the latest technical innovations, the resale value of secondhand examples was disappointing compared to foreign competitors. This was to some extent due to minor niggling problems with quality control and possibly also because the angular styling had dated far more quickly than the 1968 XJ series.

Despite so many improvements over previous Jaguar saloons, the XJ40 was always up against very stiff competition from Germany and from the 'new kid on the block', Lexus from Japan, a car engineered by Toyota and without a hint of heritage but setting standards by which all other luxury cars would be judged in the 1990s.

To address these challenges, Jaguar invested a massive £200 million of its new master Ford's money in a completely new model. Despite having to use the same floorpan, it was able to design a brand new curvaceous style for the new XJ Series (code-named X-300). Every external body panel was all-new and, although

undoubtedly deriving some inspiration from the Series 3 XJ saloons of the early 1980s, it was at once modern, striking and definitively Jaguar.

As well as recapturing its Jaguar roots, the new XJ had to be better built yet cheaper to make than its predecessor. In this the X-300 undoubtedly succeeded: for example, with 11 per cent less metal required and improved production engineering, it was both considerably cheaper to make and had a noticeably superior panel fit.

Retaining the centre section proportions of the old XJ40, the X-300 had a new prominent headlight treatment with a widened radiator grille, colour-coded bumpers, deeply sculpted bonnet and a rounded-off boot, all helping to enhance the 'softer' appeal of the styling.

Other features were new-style flush door handles which instantly gave a better feel, a 25 per cent reduction in door gaps achieved by the use of extended 'joggle' allowing the front door to overlap the rear, door-mounted rear view mirrors that folded flat against the car to aid manoeuvrability in tight areas, and a one-piece rear pressing incorporating the roof pillars (which eliminated the unsightly XJ40 'fillet').

At launch there were no less than nine models in the new XJ range, from the standard 3.2-litre saloon through Sport, Sovereign and Daimler specifications right up to the ultra-high performance XJR, which had a supercharged 4.0-litre engine. All models had their own distinctive external treatment, Sovereigns and Daimlers with full chrome trim, Sports with extensive colour coding and the XJR with bespoke colour finishes and matt black trim. Even the wheels were selected with each range in mind, totalling ten different styles.

The XJR's supercharged engine developed no less than 326bhp and catapulted this desirable car into the record books as the fastest ever Jaguar saloon at 155mph and 0-60mph in less than 6sec.

The X-300 came with a choice of three engine sizes. There was the basic AJ16 3.2-litre unit developing 219bhp at 5100rpm, the 4.0-litre AJ16 at 249bhp at 4800rpm, the supercharged 4.0-litre with 326bhp at 5000rpm, and the top-of-the-range 6.0-litre V12 at 318bhp at 5350rpm.

The supercharged version was historic in that it was Jaguar's first production saloon to be fitted with a 'blower'. It delivered an incredible 378lb ft of torque via a Roots-type Eaton M90 mechanically driven supercharger which gave immediate response to throttle openings.

Rear view (above) shows X-300 in Daimler Double Six guise. Jaguar described the styling of its new X-300 (below) as 'retrolutionary'. In other words, it recalled the acclaimed design of the 1968 XJ6 while advancing its own themes. It was good enough to win an award for Styling Director Geoff Lawson.

Other noted technical advances for the X-300 included the fitment of ventilated rear disc brakes, ABS, and electronic traction control (switchable by the driver). A new style ZF rack and pinion steering system incorporated electronically controlled, speed sensitive feel. A total of five different ride-handling packages were also available

offering differences in anti-roll bar treatment, damper settings, ride height and wheels and tyres. The new XJs also incorporated state-of-the-art security and sound systems which again varied according to model status.

Interestingly Jaguar opted for very different marketing policies for each XJ model. The base XJ6 models were targeted at the traditional driver looking for excellent value for money, the sort of person who might otherwise buy a Rover 800, BMW 5 Series, Ford Scorpio or Mercedes C Class. Sovereign models with their higher level of trim were aimed at middle/senior management types, competing with the BMW 7 Series, Mercedes E320/S280 and Lexus. Sport versions offered an alternative to the sportier BMW 5 Series models whilst the XJR was aimed very much at the BMW M5. Finally, the Daimler badged luxury models with their 'touring' suspension package appealed to drivers of cars like the BMW 750i or Mercedes S Class.

In June 1995 Jaguar announced further refinements in the X-300 range including fitting thicker glass to reduce interior noise still further and the long-awaited fitment of a passenger side glove box while retaining the second airbag.

More significant was the announcement, at the same time, of long wheelbase versions of the X-300 incorporating an extra 5in behind the centre pillar, which provided significantly improved legroom for rear seat passengers. The long-wheelbase models from that point became standard supply on Daimler models and an extra-cost option on

The ultimate in luxury. The Daimler interior in long-wheelbase Double Six form pandered to executive tastes, with separate electrically operated rear seats, all-leather upholstery, extra legroom and masses of woodwork.

In 1995 Jaguar addressed criticisms that rear legroom was limited with its long-wheelbase saloons, available in most engine and trim configurations. This is a Jaguar Sovereign 3.2.

all Jaguars (except for the Sport and XJR versions).

Daimler Double Six lwb models also had an added standard of luxury provided by twin power operated individual rear seats with electrical adjustment for the cushions, backrests and lumbar support, as well as seat heating. A new rear centre console provided switches to operate the seats and a restyled console incorporated stowage box, hinged lid, trinket tray and twin cup holders. The rear electric seat option was also available on other long wheelbase models at extra cost. As a further advance in rear seat accommodation, rear seat passengers could even adjust the front passenger seat electrically to give themselves that extra bit of legroom! Externally lwb cars were identifiable only by the extra-length rear doors.

In October 1995, Jaguar launched its most prestigious X-300 to date, the Daimler Century. The model commemorated 100 years of the Daimler marque and was based around the long-wheelbase floorpan. It retained all the top-market specifications of the Daimler Double Six Long Wheelbase but added a number of bespoke fitments, including special exterior badging, side impact strips, sill kick plates and headrests with the embossed Daimler logo.

In the short period since launch in September 1994 the X-300 helped Jaguar to achieve record sales in all markets. It also scored a major success in the American JD Power survey in 1994, almost beating the Lexus in terms of quality and customer satisfaction, and it was voted 'Most Beautiful Car in the World' by an esteemed panel of judges in Italy, all of which bodes well for the company. With the imminent release of the XJS replacement, the Jaguar story looks set to flower into the next century.

In October 1995 a new top-of-the-range model called the Daimler Century was launched to commemorate 100 years of the marque. Special markings inside and out were features.

SPECIFICATIONS

XJ6 3.2-LITRE (1994 TO DATE)

Engine: 3239cc six-cylinder twin overhead camshaft multi-valve

Bore & stroke: 91 × 83mm

Power output: 219bhp at 5100rpm

Transmission: Four-speed electronic automatic with J-gate selection or five-speed manual

Wheelbase: 9ft 4in (284cm)/9ft 8in (295cm) lwb

Length: 16ft 5in (500cm)/16ft 9in (510cm) lwb

Width: 6ft 8in (203cm)

Height: 4ft 3in (130cm)

Weight: 35½cwt (1804kg)/37cwt (1880kg) lwb

Suspension: Front: independent, unequal length wishbones, coil springs, anti-roll bar. Rear: independent, double wishbones with driveshaft upper link, coil springs

Brakes: Four-wheel ventilated discs, ABS and yaw control, power assistance

Top speed: 138mph (221kmh)

0-60mph (96kmh): 8.9 secs

Price new: £28,950

XJ6/DAIMLER SIX 4.0-LITRE (1994 TO DATE)

As XJ6 3.2-litre except:

Engine: 3980cc

Bore & stroke: 91 × 102mm

Power output: 249bhp at 4800rpm non-supercharged/326bhp at 5000rpm supercharged

Height: 4ft 2in (127cm) Sport/XJR

Weight: 37cwt (1879kg) XJR

Top speed: 143mph (229kmh) standard/155mph (248kmh) XJR

0-60mph (96kmh): 7.8 secs/5.9 secs XJR

Price new: £42,950 (Sovereign)/£45,450 (XJR)

XJ12/DOUBLE SIX 6.0-LITRE (1994 TO DATE)

Engine: 5993cc V12 cylinder single overhead camshaft per bank

Bore & stroke: 90 × 78.5mm

Power output: 318bhp at 5350rpm

Transmission: Four-speed electronic automatic transmission with J-gate selection only

Weight: 39cwt (1980kg)

Top speed: 155mph (248kmh)

0-60mph (96kmh): 6.8 secs **Price new:** £49,950

CHAPTER TWENTY-FIVE

XJ220 AND XJR-15

With 500bhp on tap, the XJ220 laid a strong claim to being the fastest road car on earth, capable of thunderous acceleration and speeds approaching 220mph.

XJ220 (1991-94)

October 1988 was to be a very memorable month for Jaguar since it marked the public debut at the British Motor Show of the spectacular XJ220 supercar. This design concept was the brainchild of Jaguar's Chief Engineer, Jim Randle, dreamt up one Christmas at his home.

This was no idle dream, however. The XJ220 was developed as a 'project of passion' at Jaguar's Engineering Department at Whitley by a small but dedicated team working in their spare time, at least initially without even the knowledge of Jaguar's board of directors. The original concept car shown at the Motor Show utilised the Jaguar V12 engine and other components taken from the TWR racing Jaguars that had competed so courageously at Le Mans in the 1980s.

For this purpose, it was clad in a futuristic aluminium tub designed by Keith Helfet, another major force also from Whitley.

It was because the XJ220 was such a success at the Motor Show that the Jaguar board took the momentous decision (pushed on by Tom Walkinshaw of TWR) to put the car into limited production through a jointly-owned company called JaguarSport.

The production XJ220 turned out to be different in some fundamental respects to the original prototype, a situation necessitated by production practicalities. The series-produced XJ220 was smaller in size and was powered by the highly successful 3.5-litre TWR/Jaguar twin-turbo V6 alloy race engine rather than the old V12 unit. With four camshafts, double injectors, four valves per cylinder, twin air-to-air intercoolers, dry sump lubrication and catalyst, the state-of-the-art

Racing mechanicals were used virtually throughout the XJ220, including the V6 twin-turbo engine, transaxle and clutch.

Despite its semi-race specification, the XJ220 had a very comfortable interior with a dashboard which would not have looked out of place on a Ford.

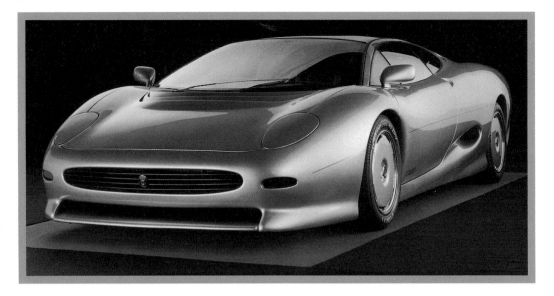

The original V12 engined show car of 1988 differed in many respects from the final production XJ220, not least of which was its much greater overall length.

Keith Helfet's original concept drawings for the V12-powered XJ220 reveal it to be an immensely long and beautiful piece of sculpture.

power plant was capable of delivering 500bhp.

The XJ220 was constructed as a bonded and riveted lightweight aerospace-style aluminium/honeycomb body with an integral chassis structure. The whole unit was then clad with alloy body panels. Aerodynamically the car drew on experience with Jaguar's Group C racers, employing front and rear aerofoils and underbody venturi effect.

Drive was to the rear wheels only via a transaxle incorporating a five-speed gearbox, spiral bevel drive and a limited slip viscous coupling differential. A twin plate 8½in AP racing clutch was required to deal with the 472lb ft torque.

With a claimed maximum speed well in excess of 200mph, the XJ220 obviously had to brake effectively. Jaguar fitted four-pot calipers on each of the massive 330mm ventilated discs. And with so much weight towards the rear, a non-assisted rack-and-pinion steering system was quite sufficient. The specially developed giant 9 × 17in front and 14 × 18in centre-lock alloy wheels were shod with ZR ultra-low profile tyres.

For its suspension the XJ220 employed Group C derived unequal length double wishbones machined from aerospace alloys. Inboard concentric coil spring/dampers, rear toe-control links and front and rear anti-roll bars ensured superlative handling.

A brand new production facility was set up by JaguarSport at Bloxham in Oxfordshire, with a dedicated workforce assembling the mechanical parts and trim. Construction of the bodies was sub-contracted to Abbey Panels, well known for their continuous production of E-type bonnets.

Jaguar set the selling price at £350,000, each buyer being expected to pay an immediate deposit of £50,000 – providing the company approved of the intending purchaser's order! In the heady late 1980s, the offers to purchase were over-subscribed and Jaguar vetted each purchaser in a half-hearted attempt to stop speculators, a ploy that didn't work!

Production eventually got underway in 1991, by which time some of the original purchasers were backing out of their 'deal', largely due to the XJ220's lack of investment potential and to general financial hardships caused by the recession. After much controversy and indeed threats of legal proceedings, most XJ220s eventually found homes, although in some cases at reduced prices. The Bloxham factory was subsequently refitted to produce the Aston Martin DB7, which was also based around many Jaguar parts.

XJ220C (1993)

In response to FISA's proposed new GT sports car category Jaguar collaborated with TWR to produce an XJ220 to competition specification in order to make it eligible to race at Le Mans and other GT series competitions.

Using technology gained from the XJR-15, the XJ220C featured composite nose, tail, door and sill sections and greatly increased accessibility to mechanical parts for pit-stops. The suspension, brakes and transaxle were all modified for race use, and the interior, mainly of Kevlar, was equipped with a digital data-logging display.

The cars were fitted with 3.5-litre V6 twin-turbo engines and other XJ220 parts, although each car was individually prepared to race and customer specification and all boasted four-wheel drive.

The zenith of the XJ220C came at the 1993 Le Mans 24 Hour race when one of the cars won the GT class in front of a crowd of thousands of enthusiastic Jaguar supporters. Due to a small infringement of the regulations, the XJ220C was sadly disqualified after the race. Nevertheless the XJ220 had scored a victory and TWR still holds the trophy!

XJR-15 (1991)

Early in 1991 a brand new Jaguar supercar was announced, code-named the XJR-15. This was effectively a development of a racing concept car known as Project R9R produced by the Jaguar/TWR joint ven-

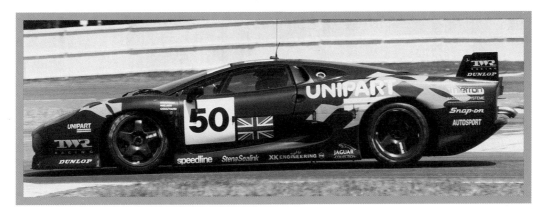

The production version of the XJ220 (above) was a handsome machine. In construction it borrowed aerospace technology and was clad in aerodynamic aluminium body panels. The gloss of the XJ220's GT class victory at Le Mans in 1993 (below) was tarnished by subsequent disqualification for a small rules infringement.

Each buyer of the 50 XJR-15s built was expected to enter perhaps the most exclusive one-make series ever. The prize?
No less than $1 million.

A brand new production line was built by Jaguar Sport at Bloxham to build the XJ220. By the time deliveries of the £400,000 car began, many speculators were trying to renege on their purchase contracts.

ture company, JaguarSport. The R9R was used as a means of testing the application of carbon composite materials and plastics in high performance vehicle construction.

The XJR-15 was based mechanically on the Le Mans 1988 winning Jaguar XJR-9, using the existing V12 engine increased to 6.0 litres and producing a massive 450bhp with a claimed top speed of over 185mph.

The concept was originally developed in 1989 and used extensively over thousands of miles to supply data back to JaguarSport for its research and future development in racing cars. At that time, Tom Walkinshaw had envisaged a unique one-make racing series to promote TWR and JaguarSport's engineering capabilities and products, so the XJR-15 seemed the ideal opportunity.

Only fifty XJR-15s were built and a pre-condition of purchase was that each owner would enter the special race series, called the Intercontinental Challenge, with an enormous $1 million prize for the winner.

The car's body and chassis were produced from lightweight composite materials such as carbon fibre and Kevlar. All mechanical parts were Jaguar-based and both designed and produced by JaguarSport, which also offered substantial back-up on and off the track for the duration of the series.

To some extent, the release of the XJR-15 undermined the impact of the XJ220, as some felt this was the car the XJ220 should have been, especially in its use of the V12 engine instead of the V6. However, the XJR-15 was designed and produced differently from the XJ220 and was never intended primarily as a road going sports car.

Some said the JaguarSport XJR-15 pulled the carpet from under the feet of the XJ220, offering stunning looks, even more exclusivity and a V12 engine, although it cost more.

The XJR-15 was a startlingly quick machine, developed as it was by TWR from the Le Mans winning XJR-9. Its 450bhp V12 engine was claimed to power the car to 185mph.

SPECIFICATIONS

XJ220 (1991-94)

Engine: 3498cc twin-turbo V6-cylinder four camshaft multi-valve
Bore & stroke: 94 × 84mm
Power output: 500bhp at 6500rpm
Transmission: Transaxle with five-speed gearbox, twin plate racing clutch
Wheelbase: 8ft 6½in (260cm)
Length: 15ft 9in (480cm)
Width: 6ft 6in (198cm)
Weight: 26½cwt (1350kg)
Suspension: Group C unequal length wishbones, inboard coil spring dampers, front and rear anti-roll bars
Brakes: Four-wheel ventilated discs with four-pot calipers
Top speed: 220mph (352kmh)
0-60mph (96kmh): 3.5 secs
Price new: £400,000 **Total Production:** 350

XJR-15 (1990-91)

Engine: 5993cc V12-cylinder single camshaft per bank
Bore & stroke: 90 × 78.5mm
Power output: 450bhp at 6250rpm
Transmission: TWR six-speed straight-cut manual
Length: 15ft 8in (478cm)
Width: 6ft 3in (190cm)
Height: 3ft 6in (107cm)
Weight: 20½cwt (1050kg)
Suspension: Front: fabricated wishbones actuating pushrods to inboard spring/damper units. Rear: alloy uprights, coil springs, dampers within wheels
Brakes: Four-wheel ventilated discs with four-pot calipers
Top speed: 185mph (300kmh)
0-60mph (96kmh): 3.5 secs
Price New: £500,000
Total Production: 50

CHAPTER TWENTY-SIX

SPECIALS & MISCELLANEOUS MODELS

The 1938 SS 100 fixed head coupé anticipated Jaguar's postwar sports car styling. Although listed as a production model, its cramped interior consigned it to history as a one-off.

It is not the intention of this publication to cover the many hundreds of specialised vehicles built around Jaguar mechanicals or rolling chassis supplied by Jaguar to outside coachbuilders for bespoke work. It is also impractical to cover the many development prototypes built by Jaguar, some of which never even saw road use. This section of the book therefore covers known examples of Jaguar's own one-offs or special specification cars, all produced by the company either for its own use or to special order.

SS 2 COMMERCIAL (CIRCA 1932)

Very little is known of two van versions of the original series SS 2 motor car that were produced by SS Cars Limited for its own use. Apparently built around the conventional chassis but with modified rear bodywork of typically angular design, the 'vans' suffered from lack of carrying space and poor payload capacity and were quickly dismantled.

SS 100 FIXED HEAD COUPE (1938)

A single vehicle based on the SS 100 3½-litre chassis was produced by SS Cars as a true fixed head coupé and was displayed at the Earls Court Motor Show in 1938.

Built by the factory to styling drawings by William Lyons himself, the car was undoubtedly very attractive with its swept-back rear end treatment, curved integral hardtop (which incorporated wind-up windows), full spats covering the rear wire wheels and curved front wings without running boards. The whole style of the car was typical of such 1930s exotics as the Bugatti Atlantique and there were strong echoes of its lines in the XK120 fixed head coupé when that was launched in 1951.

The model was even listed with a retail selling price of £595, which would have made it the most expensive SS Jaguar produced. However, no further examples were ever built as the car was found to be particularly impractical to drive due to the restricted headroom (making it difficult to enter and alight) and the awkward positioning of steering wheel and pedals. Looks, sadly, aren't everything.

The sole SS 100 fixed head coupé was eventually sold to a gentleman who spent a considerable amount of money adapting it, since when the car has changed hands many times. It still exists today after a complete restoration in the early 1980s.

The wartime VA was built for the War Department as a possible parachute drop vehicle. It used a JAP V-twin mounted on the offside rear.

More sophisticated was the VB, which used Ford Ten components and twin gearboxes, but the war was all but over by the time VB development reached its conclusion.

WARTIME GENERAL PURPOSE VEHICLES – VA AND VB (1944)

During the Second World War, SS, like many other automobile manufacturers, turned its skills and talents to the production of machinery and equipment for the war effort. As well as work for the aircraft industry, SS Cars Limited also developed two general-purpose vehicles suitable for parachute operations.

The former, VA, was a type of four-wheeled 'jeep', small and very light, powered by a JAP V-twin 1096cc air-cooled engine mounted at the offside rear of the vehicle driving a gearbox by chain.

The second, perhaps more practical vehicle, the VB, was powered by a Ford Ten engine driving through a Ford three-speed gearbox to the rear wheels; an auxiliary gearbox provided a choice of up to six forward gears. A new type of independent rear suspension was adopted (which shared some resemblance to 1960s Jaguars) and at the front conventional wishbones and coil springs were used with a hydraulic braking system.

Although a great deal of time had been devoted to the development of these two military vehicles, by the time of their release they were not needed so never went into serious production.

THE BRONTOSAURUS (1952)

And now, as they say, for something completely different! The Jaguar special of specials. This ungainly looking vehicle was the result of a collaboration between William Lyons and the famous record-breaker Goldie Gardner.

The very unusual body was made up from aluminium panels grafted on to an ash wooden frame in

The aptly-named Brontosaurus was built in aluminium over a C-type chassis. It was intended to be an aerodynamic record breaker, but it never got the chance to prove its mettle.

the time-honoured coachbuilder's fashion and styled for maximum aerodynamic efficiency. Underneath all that bodywork was a conventional C-type car including all mechanicals and even its wheels.

Originally conceived merely as a design concept, William Lyons himself sanctioned the construction of a running car, although it never actually took to a public road but was merely driven around the Browns Lane factory until it was decided to break it up. It was probably his intention to consider some sort of record-breaking attempt with the car or even a form of racing. Another project at the around the same time explored the possibility of Jaguar entering Formula 1, although this too never came to fruition.

MARK VII CONVERTIBLES (CIRCA 1950)

Several attempts were made, mainly by outside coachbuilders, to produce specialist bodywork on the Mark VII chassis, including hearse bodies and even the odd estate car.

Jaguar itself built two convertibles which would have taken over the role of the Mark V Drophead Coupé. Both were effectively conventional Mark VIIs with the roof cut off, and one was adapted with two-door bodywork. The other also received a contemporary American electric ram hood mechanism.

The Mark VII convertible never came to production, mainly due to the success of the saloon version but also probably due to the prohibitive cost of development and limited production possibilities. Both cars were apparently scrapped by the factory and sadly no photographs remain.

MARK VII – ROYAL PATRONAGE (1954)

Her Majesty the Queen Mother took a shine to the Jaguar Mark VII saloon and, after a drive in one of the factory cars, decided to place a special order.

Her 1954 example was supplied on permanent loan to the Queen Mother and was essentially a standard production car suitably equipped with West of England cloth covers for the rear seating, separate radio controls in the rear compartment, additional vanity mirrors set in the doors and other minor changes. The Queen Mother enjoyed driving herself and so the car, an automatic, was also specially adapted with a large horn push button on the top dashboard cant rail so that the right hand could be easily dropped from the steering wheel to the horn.

Over the years the car was regularly returned to Jaguar for maintenance and updating, which included conversion to Mark IX specification complete with disc brakes, chromium-plated radiator grille and even a one-piece windscreen.

The Queen Mother finally handed the Mark VII back to the factory in 1974, at which time a commemorative plaque was attached to the dashboard. Since then the car has been retained for static exhibition and the occasional run, and has now become part of the Jaguar-Daimler Heritage Trust collection.

E1A (1957)

E1A was very much a prototype for the E-type sports car, built with an aluminium body of similar construction to the early D-types in 1957 but with generally slightly smaller dimensions. Using magnesium alloy for the supporting framework and monocoque construction, the now well-known forward-hinged one-piece bonnet section was used at the front, with stressed rear bodywork.

Because of its smaller size, E1A was powered by the 2.4-litre version of the XK engine and used one of Jaguar's first designs of independent rear suspension, but without the supportive subframe later used on production cars. E1A was totally roadworthy even down to the fitment of side-screens; however, there were no headlights (only side lights) nor any windscreen wipers! E1A was used extensively as a testbed for the E-type on and off public roads but was unfortunately later broken up.

E2A (1958)

E2A was a further development vehicle for the E-type but with much more practical uses in mind. Designed as a sports-racing car, it was considered a possible

This prototype, called E1A, was built in aluminium in 1957. Many E-type elements can be seen, but the lines were more bulbous and a 2.4-litre XK engine was fitted.

E2A was another E-type precursor and was intended as a sports-racing successor to the D-type. As such it used many D-type elements and can be regarded as a D/E cross-over car.

Dripping with 24-carat gold, this extraordinary Mark 2 was Jaguar's star exhibit at the 1960 New York Motor Show. Absolutely every item of brightwork was gold-plated.

replacement for the D-type as a Le Mans racer in the late 1950s.

E2A looked remarkably similar to the E-type and was of virtually the same dimensions. With a decidedly E-type frontal aspect, although without the power bulge in the bonnet, E2A also featured a 'proper' windscreen but retained many aspects of the D-type rear end and, of course, the peg drive Dunlop wheels.

Mechanically E2A was a mix of cars, using a 3-litre version of the dry sump lubricated XK engine, with an alloy block and Lucas fuel injection, which developed 293bhp at 6750rpm. A four-speed all-synchromesh gearbox with triple plate clutch was employed with cross-over D-/E-type front suspension and totally independent rear suspension, although again without the subframe or trailing radius arms of the production E-type.

It lay around at Jaguar for some time, and eventually Briggs Cunningham from America convinced Jaguar to let him race the car. It was painted in American white-and-blue colours for the 1960 Le Mans 24 Hour race, where it retired after constant fuel injection problems and finally a blown cylinder head gasket.

Jaguar later fitted a 3.8-litre XK engine with Weber carburettors and a power bulge bonnet. The car was subsequently sent to America, where it was campaigned with relative success until retired back to England. E2A then joined a private collection where it still resides today.

THE GOLDEN MARK 2 (1960)

To captivate the North American market after the very successful launch of the Mark 2 saloon in 1959, Jaguar

The Mark 2 was not only a favourite of villains – the police recognised its dynamic qualities too. Jaguar supplied them with specially prepared Mark 2s, although generally these were untouched mechanically.

attended the 1960 New York motor show with a rather special version of the 3.8-litre saloon.

A standard production car was taken from the assembly line, finished in Old English White with magnolia leather interior. All the brightwork was removed to be gold-plated especially for the show. The gold-plated trim included literally everything from mascot to wiper arms, side light surrounds to rain gutters. Even the wire wheels were finished in gold plate!

Set off with white-walled tyres, this $25,000 car was displayed with a fashion model wearing a specially commissioned 24 carat gold-threaded gown and tiara which contained over 1000 diamonds.

The car was later returned to Jaguar where the gold was 'de-commissioned', and the car was eventually sold off as a normal production 3.8-litre saloon.

MARK 2 POLICE SPECIFICATION (1960s)

Whilst Jaguar had become renowned for supplying various British police forces with vehicles from the 1930s on, nearly all of these cars were standard production vehicles merely fitted with up-rated batteries to accommodate radio equipment. Jaguar first started to 'advertise' the supply of specialist vehicles for the police with the Mark 1 in the late 1950s but it was not until the introduction of the Mark 2 in 1959 that a special Police Specification model became available.

The specially prepared Mark 2s featured a number of modifications to make them as practical as possible for police use, such as the removal of the back seat to accommodate warning signs, lighting and so on, the replacement of carpeting with non-slip rubber matting, and in some cases the removal of door trims, replaced by simple painted hardboard. Dashboards were equipped with provision for radio equipment and a calibrated observer speedometer plus an auxiliary switch panel for warning lights, siren and loud-hailer systems.

Contrary to popular belief, most Mark 2 Police Specification vehicles were not 'souped up', merely relying on the standard 3.8-litre engine, perhaps with a close-ratio gearbox and uprated rear springing to assist the additional load carrying needs.

MARK 2 COUNTY ESTATE CAR (1962)

Jaguar never actually produced an estate car derivative of any of its normal saloons although several outside coachbuilders attempted work on Mark Vs, VIIs and others. Nor did Jaguar actually produce the Mark 2 County Estate covered here, but it was a vehicle that it purchased and seriously considered producing in vol-

Dashboard of the police specification Mark 2 had provision for a radio. Note the stripped-out nature of the trim.

Duncan Hamilton and Mike Hawthorn inspired the Mark 2 County estate, used by Jaguar as a race support vehicle.

ume, so it is worthy of inclusion in this chapter.

Duncan Hamilton and Mike Hawthorn were both factory race drivers in the 1950s in C-types and D-types. Jaguar mostly used Mark VII saloons as tenders for the supply of spares, tyres and so on, driven by the team of mechanics accompanying the race cars on their outings. The idea of a small Jaguar estate car to fulfil this role came from these two drivers. They tried to get Sir William Lyons interested in the project but he unfortunately showed little enthusiasm.

In the end an outside coachbuilder, Jones Brothers Limited, was commissioned to build a vehicle based on styling exercises supplied by the drivers and others. The finished vehicle, based around a 3.8-litre Mark 2, was quite an attractive and usable alternative to the standard saloon.

Jaguar purchased the County Estate (as it was dubbed) and used it extensively as part of the race and rally entourage, during which time it endured quite a hard life. The prospect of a production version, however, never proceeded any further and eventually the County was sold off into private hands. Although passing through several owners, being 'lost' at one time, and then going overseas, the car is still in existence today. It is possible, although not confirmed, that a second example may have also been produced.

LIGHTWEIGHT E-TYPES (1963)

After some encouraging successes in 1961 and 1962 with racing E-types, Jaguar was persuaded to build a limited run of 'competition' models, with improved performance and reduced weight the main criteria. As the cars were all individually prepared there was no definitive specification; however there was a common basis for the concept.

Bodily the whole monocoque, along with inner and outer panelling, was crafted entirely in aluminium instead of steel and all cars had fixed hard-tops, again in aluminium (instead of glassfibre) which contributed to the overall strength of the vehicle.

For the suspension the front end retained much of the production E-type specification although with stiffer torsion and anti-roll bars, uprated shock absorbers and special upper and lower fulcrum housings. At the rear the E-type system was used, with modifications including a stiffer cage bottom plate, lightened hub carriers, modified wishbones and mountings, shock absorbers with integral bump-stops and 25 per cent stiffer mountings. Some cars featured the conventional Power-Lok differential while others had ZF or Thornton units. Larger disc brakes were fitted, with uprated calipers and servo, and there were 15in Dunlop peg drive wheels.

The engine used for the 'competition' E-types was the most highly developed yet; of 3.8 litres capacity it had an alloy block with a special wide-angled cylinder head incorporating Lucas mechanical fuel injection. Engines developed between 320 and 344bhp dependent on final spec and in most cases were mated to a ZF five-speed manual gearbox.

Twelve true Lightweights were built and although several other E-types were also released for competition work these did not necessarily have the aluminium monocoque. Today many of these Lightweight E-types survive and a number of specialist companies have built accurate replicas.

XJ6 SERIES 1 COUPÉ (1971)

The series-produced Jaguar XJ Coupé was introduced in the mid-1970s. However, information has recently come to light of an older Coupé, based on a 4.2-litre Series 1 short-wheelbase bodyshell, which was produced by Jaguar as a prototype for the Series 2.

The car is primarily Series 1 except for the roof section, two-door treatment and windows. It found its way to Australia where it was recently unearthed and restored to its former glory. This is the only known example of a Series 1 XJ Coupé.

XJ SERIES 2 COUPÉ BROADSPEED RACERS (1976/77)

Jaguar's direct involvement in competition ended with the D-types but, with the introduction of the XJ Coupé, British Leyland decided to launch an assault on the European Touring Car Championship.

Ralph Broad of Broadspeed Engineering had previously shown an interest in developing a racing Jaguar V12, and he was commissioned to design and build the car around a conventional Coupé monocoque.

The V12 engine was bored out to 5416cc, with a 12:1 compression ratio, Lucas fuel injection and a conventional Jaguar four-speed close-ratio gearbox with single plate clutch. With massive four-pot caliper disc brakes (initially water-cooled) and expensively manufactured precision wheels to withstand the tremendous cornering pressures, the 'Big Cat', as it became known, took six months to develop and made its debut at Easter 1976.

Two examples were fielded for most races but the lack of sufficient development and the probability that the Coupé body was just too big to go racing resulted in the racers' complete withdrawal at the end of 1977. The two cars are still in the hands of Jaguar and are currently undergoing partial refurbishment by the Jaguar-Daimler Heritage Trust.

XJS LONG WHEELBASE (CIRCA 1980)

The XJS had been a successful car for Jaguar since its introduction in 1975 and the company was keen to build on this success. The product planners accordingly tried several variations on the theme to expand the market for the XJS.

The first attempt was to produce a long-wheelbase version of the model, still maintaining the two-door, four-seat layout but with the same wheelbase as an XJ saloon model. An example was put together using a modified Jaguar Series 3 saloon roof panel, and the one and only long-wheelbase XJS was left to deteriorate outdoors for a number of years without any further development, finally being broken up quite recently.

DAIMLER XJS (CIRCA 1984)

An intriguing variation of the XJS came with the production of a Daimlerised version produced to evaluate

Jaguar built 'Lightweight' racing E-types with aluminium bodywork, modified suspension, uprated brakes and highly developed 3.8-litre XK engines tuned to customer order.

One genuine Series 1 XJ Coupé was built as a precursor to the production Series 2 Coupe. It has recently been restored in Australia.

The infamous XJ Coupé Broadspeed racer with its fantastically widened wheelarches and air dam. It was too heavy and fragile to be a consistent front-runner.

Styling drawing for the proposed Series 1 XJ Coupé shown in the photograph above. Not much is known of the story of this exercise.

The Daimler Double Six S was an intriguing experiment. Based on a Cabriolet, it would have been an alternative fixed head style to the XJS. There is even a fluted grille!

the possibility of a new market for such a car, which was to be called the Daimler Double Six S.

A standard XJS Cabriolet was taken from the production line and suitably modified with a Daimler fluted radiator grille and rear boot panel, the addition of Daimler and Double Six badging and revised wheels. The big change came in the roof section: the twin Cabriolet targa panels were sealed and made up in steel and the rear hood section was replaced by a steel panel incorporating the rear side windows and rear heated screen, the whole roof assembly then being painted in body colour, in this particular case metallic blue.

Inside, the Daimler had walnut veneer, Daimler badging and rear seating from the conventional XJS fixed head.

Although the model never reached series production, it is understood that since the Daimler's existence has become known several hopeful purchasers have placed specific orders for a Daimler XJS! The original car is now in the hands of the Jaguar-Daimler Heritage Trust.

XJ40 ESTATE CAR (1992)

A couple of XJ40 saloons were converted to estate cars by independent coachbuilders and the execution seemed a natural progression – in fact some said the design of the estate was more harmonious than the saloon! With the luxury estate car market firmly in the hands of marques like Mercedes-Benz and BMW, Jaguar seriously considered producing a competitor to expand sales of the XJ40.

A single XJ40 estate car was made in 1992, finished in silver and built to 4.0-litre Sovereign specification. It was regularly driven by several Jaguar directors including Managing Director Nick Scheele himself. No attempt was made to keep the car secret; in fact several magazines featured photographs of the car

along with comments from Jaguar on the vehicle. It appeared that Jaguar actually wanted people to know about the car to assess public opinion.

Evidently the response was disappointing for no Jaguar estate car ever materialised in production. The XJ40 one-off is now officially part of the Jaguar-Daimler Heritage Trust.

XJ40 TWO-DOOR COUPÉ (1993)

Another deviation from the saloon car theme came in 1992/93 with the construction of a one-off two-door coupé design on the existing XJ40 body style. Again based on a Sovereign, this time finished in Bordeaux red, the exercise was kept relatively secret until the arrival of the new X-300.

The car was very attractively styled, retaining much of the XJ40 shape, although with larger doors and a more stylish side/rear window treatment. Again nothing further came of the project but it is reasonable to assume that, at some time in the future, Jaguar will once again follow in the footsteps of the Series 2 XJ Coupé and produce an up-to-date luxurious two-door variant on the X-300 saloon floorpan to compete with BMW and Mercedes.

Good-looking XJ40 Coupe was another factory one-off, killed because the X-300 was imminent.

This 1992 estate version of the XJ40 was a serious production possibility. However, load height was quite high and in any case the XJ40 was nearing the end of its life.

Cut-down rear seats do not disguise the fact that accommodation in the coupé's rear was drastically reduced by the shortening of the wheelbase.

ACKNOWLEDGEMENTS

The author and the publisher are grateful to the following for providing photographs reproduced in this book:

Classic and Sportscar (Haymarket Magazines), *Classic Cars* (IPC Magazines), David Hodges, Mark Hughes, Jaguar Cars, Jaguar-Daimler Heritage Trust, Chris Rees.